THE SIX NEW RULES OF BUSINESS

The Six
NEW RULES of
BUSINESS

Creating Real Value in a Changing World

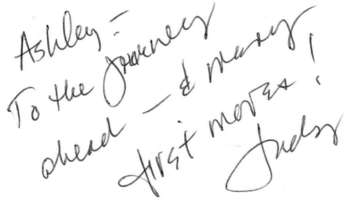

Ashley =
To the journey
ahead — & many
first movers !
Judy

JUDY SAMUELSON

BK®

Berrett–Koehler Publishers, Inc.

Berrett-Koehler Publishers, Inc.
1333 Broadway, Suite 1000
Oakland, CA 94612-1921
Tel: (510) 817-2277
Fax: (510) 817-2278
www.bkconnection.com

ORDERING INFORMATION
Quantity sales. Special discounts are available on quantity purchases by corporations, associations, and others. For details, contact the "Special Sales Department" at the Berrett-Koehler address above.

Individual sales. Berrett-Koehler publications are available through most bookstores. They can also be ordered directly from Berrett-Koehler: Tel: (800) 929-2929; Fax: (802) 864-7626; www.bkconnection.com.

Orders for college textbook/course adoption use. Please contact Berrett-Koehler: Tel: (800) 929-2929; Fax: (802) 864-7626.

Distributed to the U.S. trade and internationally by Penguin Random House Publisher Services.

Berrett-Koehler and the BK logo are registered trademarks of Berrett-Koehler Publishers, Inc.

Printed in the United States of America

Berrett-Koehler books are printed on long-lasting acid-free paper. When it is available, we choose paper that has been manufactured by environmentally responsible processes. These may include using trees grown in sustainable forests, incorporating recycled paper, minimizing chlorine in bleaching, or recycling the energy produced at the paper mill.

Library of Congress Cataloging-in-Publication Data
Names: Samuelson, Judy, author.
Title: The six new rules of business : creating real value in a changing
    world / Judy Samuelson.
Description: First edition. | Oakland, CA : Berrett-Koehler Publishers,
    [2020] | Includes index.
Identifiers: LCCN 2020033251 | ISBN 9781523089963 (hardcover ; alk. paper)
    | ISBN 9781523089970 (adobe pdf) | ISBN 9781523089987 (epub)
Subjects: LCSH: Organizational change. | Corporate culture. | Strategic
    planning. | Success in business.
Classification: LCC HD58.8 .S25944 2020 | DDC 658—dc23
LC record available at https://lccn.loc.gov/2020033251

First Edition
26 25 24 23 22 21 20   10 9 8 7 6 5 4 3 2 1

Book production: Linda Jupiter Productions; *Text design:* Kim Scott, Bumpy Design;
Cover design: Nola Burger; *Edit:* Elissa Rabellino; *Proofread:* Mary Kanable;
Index: Paula C. Durbin-Westby

To Lynn Stout (1957–2018)—whose scholarship and teaching about corporate governance and fiduciary duty opened our minds about corporate *purpose*—and to the many scholars and advocates she mentored who will go the next mile.

The future is already here—it is just not very evenly distributed.

—WILLIAM GIBSON

Contents

Preface

None of the major problems confronting the globe today—
sustainability, health care, poverty, financial-system repair—
can be solved unless business plays a significant role.
—NITIN NOHRIA, DEAN, HARVARD BUSINESS SCHOOL

IT WAS DURING MY TIME at the Ford Foundation that I began to think concretely about corporations and the role and influence of the private sector.

In 1995, at a meeting of the foundation's trustees, I was asked a question for which I didn't have an answer: *Why doesn't anyone at the Ford Foundation talk about business?* The capacities and resources of the companies led by some of the foundation's trustees dwarfed our own: Cummins Engine, Levi Strauss, Reuters, Tata, Xerox. *Could we better enlist business in our work?*

It was a nose-under-the-tent moment from which I've never pulled back.

My colleagues and I began to study businesses that had followed a path or had a track record that connected with the foundation's mission of economic development. The business leaders we took note of in 1995 were influenced by myriad forces—from the personal to the political. Something had caused each of them to embrace the social impacts of their business model. They saw business opportunity in unusual places. A catalytic event or regulation or strong vision or moral code enabled a kind of business and society thinking that aligned a part of their operations or capital with the health of the commons.

At Levi Strauss, the founding family's values supported long-term investment in the communities where it manufactured jeans. Bank of America was brought to the table by the Community Reinvestment Act, a law passed in 1977 that required banks to reinvest in communities where they sourced deposits; community bankers began to understand the mechanics and strategy behind targeted lending to support the real economic potential of the inner city. An aggressive NGO-led campaign forced Nike to scrub its supply chain of sweatshop labor practices, which in turn inspired the company to go the extra mile and raise the bar on its industry and competitors. Texas Instruments found competitive advantage in a racially diverse workforce that mirrored the demographics of its state—and its future customers.

In each case, the mindset or personal engagement of the chief executive was instrumental in aligning the culture with creation of real business value. By moral code or necessity, or both, they were able to overcome, or interpret differently, the single objective function of profit maximization to consider both long-term risk and opportunity.

It was as if these leaders were playing the game by a different set of rules.

Today the pace of change in business is dizzying. It exposes reputational fault lines for companies that stick with the old rules. Dynamic forces—from Internet-powered transparency to profound changes in the role of capital to the complexity of global exchange of goods and services—conspire to clarify the new rules of value creation and put the old rules to rest.

Business is the most influential institution of our day. We need business's talent, investment, problem-solving skills, and global reach to make progress on intractable problems from climate change to inequality to equipping workers for a new age of work. This lens on business does not override the need for government regulation and public investment. Indeed, business is a powerful influencer of public policy as well. To what ends is business using its voice?

In 2018, Larry Fink, founder and chief executive of BlackRock, the world's largest asset management company, called for CEOs to consider the public purpose of their enterprises. He was echoing decades of work by scholars and advocates, posing a near-timeless question: Why do we grant corporations the license to operate? Fink's consistent message demonstrates just how much the rules of the game have changed in the last decade—and especially since economist Milton Friedman proclaimed profit seeking and returns to shareholders the organizing principle of the corporation.

Friedman has a long shadow. He and his acolytes were so successful in their quest to reorient managers that by the early 2000s, over 90 percent of earnings for the public companies in the S&P 500 were redistributed to owners of stock in the form of share buybacks and dividends rather than invested in expansion or awarded to the employees who bore real risk of business failure. Short-term noise in the markets and simplistic financial models ensured that a range of critical business issues that were threats to social stability and the biosphere stayed confined to the ethics classroom. Our vision of business is crowded with stories of greed laced with short-term thinking, from Wells Fargo to Purdue Pharma, VW to Boeing.

Yet, as we step into the ecosystem of business today, we experience profound change in attitudes and a new kind of business vision. The new rules are utilized both by employees driving change within and by sophisticated NGOs that target global brands vulnerable to extended supply chains. The rules are also making headway in boardrooms animated by self-interest—even self-preservation—from the war for talent to the quest for a reliable supply chain to the reality of a changing climate. *The new rules have staying power.*

This book is for executives, but also for those who advise business leaders or aim to influence business corporations, in order to repair damage done and ensure that business is fit for the future. In the first six chapters, we explore six trends—six new rules—and the forcing functions that are picking up the pace of change. The instruments of change are forged by the tech-and-social-media-enabled collective voice, which in turn amplifies risk, opportunity, and shifting business imperatives. Norms that influence the mindset and instincts of business leaders unquestionably have shifted, but there is still work to do. In chapters 7 and 8, we look at the road ahead—the parts of the system that reinforce the status quo and are most resistant to change.

What is needed now are a fundamental rethinking of the decision rules and a breaking down of old norms that are holding us back, from how finance classrooms teach valuation to how executives are compelled to focus on the stock price through incentives and rewards. Design for the future requires business models that value the real contributors—including workers *and* nature—and that pay dividends on the public's license to operate.

The new rules of business are the starting point for restoring trust in an institution that contributes immeasurably to much that we take for granted and depend on. The new rules are the key to real value creation and a sustainable future.

The Cost of Ignoring the New Rules of Real Value Creation

It's all a question of story. We are in trouble just now because we do not have a good story. We are in between stories. The Old Story—the account of how the world came to be and how we fit into it—is not functioning properly, and we have not learned the New Story.
—THOMAS BERRY, "THE NEW STORY"

IN 1999, THE *NEW YORK TIMES* chronicled the egregious behavior of the Royal Caribbean cruise line. The company, founded in Norway but based in Florida, was censored for dumping toxic waste and spent fuel in the Caribbean Sea and US coastal waters, endangering the coral reefs, beaches, and sea life that their customers book passage to enjoy.

Before ships set sail, the waste containment system is inspected, so the dumping was clearly intentional. Dumping spent fuel lightens the load, saves fuel costs, and avoids waste disposal fees back in port. It also endangers the ecosystem and is a clear violation of the public trust. The actions for which Royal Caribbean was censured put both the company's long-term interests and reputation at risk.

What was the ship engineer thinking? Why risk tarnishing your own brand to save money today?

A TALE OF A SYSTEM GONE WRONG: FROM ROYAL CARIBBEAN TO BOEING

Fast-forward to 2016, when James Robert Liang became the first Volkswagen employee to admit guilt in the company's rogue program to undermine government emission standards. For Liang and others at VW, the constraints on emissions signaled the need to innovate—not by building a better diesel engine, but by designing and installing software to fake the real emission levels during testing.

The VW story was shocking when it broke, but also mystifying. How long did they expect to keep the deception secret? By the time of Liang's admission of guilt, the company had already paid out $15 billion in penalties and even greater claims, and lawsuits were piling up in both the United States and the far larger European market.

And Boeing may never fully recover from the deadly consequences of a culture driving too hard toward the bottom line. In April 2020, as the coronavirus roiled the airline industry, Boeing announced that customers had canceled orders for 150 of its best-selling plane, the 737 Max. By then, the plane had been grounded for over a year as the company worked to fix the ill-designed operating system that was linked to two airline crashes—hundreds of lives, and the trust of pilots in Boeing itself, destroyed. The sidelining of those assets resulted in hundreds of flights being canceled each day at the peak of the 2019 summer travel season. A $4.9 billion charge against earnings was just the first step in assessing the cost of the business failure—the opening pitch in the game of blame and valuation of lives lost that will proceed over years, if not decades.

Tell me which of the pressing issues of our time keep you awake at night, and I will tell you how the old rules of profit maximization and short-term thinking contribute to those problems.

Globe-hopping brands with big footprints and deep supply chains and the extensive reach of industry, technology, and commerce touch virtually every aspect of our lives. Climate change is a product of industrial processes. It is a problem with unimaginable consequences that cannot be solved without collective action; it now tops the list of global concerns. We can easily connect the dots between consumers shopping on the basis of price, low-cost labor markets, and the working conditions where human rights violations and even human trafficking persist. The economics of overconsumption and unsustainable growth create boom-and-bust cycles that favor some but push others to the side. Marketing of unhealthy products. Tax avoidance. Obesity. Our infatuation with guns. Food waste. Deforestation. Pervasive inequality and its consequences.

For good or for ill (and it's both), global business—talent-rich, capacious, and connected—is the most influential institution of our age, akin to the Church in the Middle Ages. Clues to the power of business are found in daily headlines and in politics.

We need a new script.

This book offers a different—and more useful—set of rules that can transform the game of business. And it provides stories about how the game is already changing according to the new rules.

The rules followed by corporations aren't set in one place, like the Vatican. They emerge from Congress, regulatory agencies, and trade associations. They are set by investors with different time frames and definitions of a fair return on investment (ROI), and by outside activists, internal agitators, and purchasing agents who are under pressure to redefine the narrative about business success. *But, ultimately, they emerge from business itself*—they are a function of embedded assumptions, decision rules, protocols, and incentive systems that shape intentions and behavior.

Yet, it is also true that the rules and expectations that companies choose to follow are unquestionably tied to the belief that shareholders own the firm and that clarity of managing to a single objective of shareholder value leaves us all better off. The evidence to the contrary is overwhelming, but systems change is hard, especially when the ideology is reinforced by the tenure system in classrooms and myriad forces in boardrooms.

The old rules derive from the power of the shareholder mindset. The new ones are derivative of the change that is enabled when other, more powerful contributors to value creation are revealed. The threads of this conversation about corporate purpose are woven throughout the rules that mark the chapters of this book.

The underlying narrative about the purpose of the corporation, and the practices and mindset that give shareholder primacy its power, are giving way, at last, to the reality that business and society are truly codependent. New, future-oriented sources of power and influence are already affecting the game, and a new cadre of business leaders are redefining business success. Business schools are catching up with boardrooms wrestling with a new road map—one that points the way to new measures of progress and is consistent with the values of the new generation preparing to lead.

THE COST OF IGNORING THE NEW RULES OF VALUE CREATION

The stories of Royal Caribbean, and VW and Boeing, follow a similar line. To dump waste carries some risk, but it is guaranteed to reduce the cost of doing business and keep prices low to consumers. The ship's engineer was likely rewarded for finding a way to cut costs. The engineers at VW cared about the environment, but the rules and incentives that defined the culture were principally designed to grow market share. Boeing scuttled protocols and silenced contrary voices in the campaign to beat Airbus. Wells Fargo maxed revenues by creating the conditions for account managers to push products onto unwitting customers. Goldman Sachs and JPMorgan Chase created innovative securities for the mortgage market that purported to shield investors from risk (they did not) and helped fuel the housing bubble and subsequent mortgage meltdown of 2008.

And before all of these examples became front-page news, there was Enron, a high-performing stock in the late '90s that proved to be a house of cards and spectacularly collapsed in 2001.

Enron failed several years into the design of a program I founded in 1998 with a grant from the Ford Foundation to support fresh thinking about the role of corporations in both classrooms and boardrooms. I chose the Aspen Institute, founded by a Chicago industrialist in 1949 and known for problem-solving through dialogue and leadership development, as the program's home.

A decade earlier, in 1989, I had left a job at Bankers Trust as a lender to manufacturers and importers of apparel to join Ford's Program-Related Investments division. As the head of Ford's venture in what today would be called "impact investing," I oversaw a $100 million portfolio of loans and investments structured to encourage banks and insurance companies, from Allstate to Bank of America, to coinvest in community-based economic development.

My territory at Ford was a big leap from New York's garment center. I visited US-operated factories in El Paso's neighboring city Juarez, Mexico, and villages in Bangladesh experimenting with microcredit, as well as US locations from Arkansas to rural Maine to inner-city Cleveland. The globally astute members of the foundation's board included corporate titans like David Kearns of Xerox, Ratan Tata of Tata Industries, Henry Schacht of Cummins Engine, and Bob Haas of Levi Strauss.

These trustees were at home with the intentions of the program and didn't question the risks we took. Instead, they posed questions that caused us to consider a peculiar divide between the foundation's work and its origins. We were investing and spending Henry Ford's vast wealth without pausing to think about how it had been created.

With seven years of banking under my belt, I understood that at Ford we were working in the shadows of business but without directly considering the private sector's role and impact on the foundation's mission of expanding economic opportunity in the United States and globally.

When I began the Business and Society Program at the Aspen Institute, we started by probing the connections between how leaders think about their responsibilities and the attitudes imparted by teaching in business classrooms. It was the heyday of the MBA; rising executives all seemed to come through business schools.

The demise of Enron seemed to happen overnight. It occurred while my colleagues and I were testing a format for dialogue among business leaders that over several years included Ken Lay, the CEO of Enron; and executives from Shell, McKinsey, PwC, BlackRock, General Dynamics, Cummins Engine, and Pepsi. As we headed home to New York from our conference center in Aspen, Colorado, the attacks on the Twin Towers reverberated through the markets and permanently reset our worldview.

The events that followed from the World Trade Center on September 11, 2001, and the failure of Enron that fall will always be conflated in my mind. Enron died by a host of decisions that enabled it to dominate key markets and to prop up earnings per share. The old rules of profit maximization that governed Enron enriched some but ultimately failed all of us.

It's time for a new set of rules.

The old rules paid off, at least for a while. This book is about the changes—the forces that are conspiring both inside businesses and in the business ecosystem—that enable executives to think and manage differently. It is about the consequences for businesses that fail to embrace the new rules, and a new definition of business success.

Sociologists talk about the scripts that guide human behavior—the interplay of intentions and decisions that look obscene when exposed but are, in fact, cultural norms. The engineers and professionals and managers at Enron, VW, and Boeing were not malcontents laying the seeds of the company's own destruction; they were operating within the protocols of their companies and within highly competitive industries.

Public capital markets are complicit. With all of the attention paid to so-called socially responsible investors, the stock price still falls when a business invests in public goods—for example, when a tech company announces that it is adding jobs; or a drug company spends on R&D without an immediate payback; or a consumer product company, like Pepsi, or a retailer, like CVS or Walmart, reduces its exposure to a product with a profound social cost that contributes a lot to the bottom line. When Pepsi cut marketing budgets for regular soda to make room for "good for you" drinks and snacks, it paid the price on Wall Street. In chapter 3, we see that Pepsi ultimately gave in to these pressures but continued to build a portfolio of healthier products for which it is also known.

The playing field is complex. But *the corporation itself is not moral or immoral*—it is not good or bad like a person—rather, the decisions made by the company are what have good or bad results. And the decisions are a function of the rules and incentives and metrics that influence behavior in the executive suite and on the shop floor. The rules are set by leaders—they reflect what the leaders believe to be true and what they value. To move the needle on the problems that keep us awake at night, to break this vicious circle, we need to change how business leaders—and their counterparts in finance—think and act.

In the early 2000s, in the wake of Enron's demise, the highly respected dean of the Kellogg School of Management, Don Jacobs, announced a new screening process to weed out the "bad apples" before they enrolled. But we don't fix the system by closing the gates at Kellogg or Harvard, or by sending midlevel engineers from VW or top executives of Enron to prison, as necessary or satisfying as that may be. We need to unravel the rules of the road under which the decisions of the executives of Enron—and a host of players revealed since—make sense.

The first step is to look deeply into the business system and how the core assumptions and dominant beliefs—the mindset of the executive—are shaped and reinforced and in turn shape the incentives for the middle managers, the engineers, and the CFOs.

NEW RULES: REAL VALUE

Chapter 1 examines the first of six new rules that are already influencing these assumptions and the conduct of business. Behind Rule

#1 is the growth in intangible forms of value, from employee know-how and loyalty to a firm's reputation and license to operate. These assets are difficult to measure and upset traditional valuation formulas and measures. The measurement of real value connects the company to the natural and human ecosystem on which it depends: the consequences of decisions today on future generations cannot be discounted. Embedded in the understanding of future value—real sustained value—are risks that are easy to ignore today.

Chapter 2 explores the profound shifts taking place as the organizing principle of "shareholder value" gives way to common-sense management behind Rule #2—the reality that companies naturally serve many different objectives in order to flourish. Decades of probing both theory and practice in the work of Lynn Stout, Marty Lipton, Ira Millstein, Lynn Paine, Leo Strine, and other important voices have succeeded, at last, in disrupting the belief that corporate law, aka the laws of Delaware, where many public companies are incorporated, requires public companies to manage the company as if the shareholders own the enterprise itself, rather than shares of stock with specific rights.

These new rules pave the way for business decisions oriented to the future. Importantly, these new rules depend on forms of corporate accountability proving to be more powerful than adherence to shareholder preferences.

Yet, two decades after Enron's implosion, we are still experiencing the consequences of decades of teaching, as well as the strategic advice aimed at profit or share price as the principal—even single—objective of a well-run business. The old rule of profit maximization is giving way to more critical measures of real value. It is also true that the scaffolding that supports the shareholder mindset is still firmly in place.

The purpose of the enterprise is determined by the board and executive, but, importantly, it is also revealed in how the leaders act—in the choices they consider.

Assumptions and incentives that underpin shareholder primacy have developed a language and narrative of their own. Statements like "pay for performance" and "maximize shareholder value" are spoken as if they were handed down with the Ten Commandments. The drumbeat about shareholder primacy, and performance measures such as total shareholder return (TSR), feed short-term-oriented investors at the expense of employees, stewardship of natural resources, and constructive engagement with host communities.

These inputs are the source of real business value.

Adam Kahane, author of *Solving Tough Problems: An Open Way of Talking, Listening, and Creating New Realities*, facilitated our first Business Leader Dialogue as the seeds of Enron's destruction were being revealed. Adam uses a form of scenario planning he learned at Royal Dutch Shell to build the will for change in difficult environments. He would start our dialogues with the following thought: *"The system is perfectly designed for the result we have now—if we want a different result, we need to rethink the system."*

As classrooms and boardrooms move to a more coherent and useful conception of fiduciary duty, new questions emerge:

- ◆ Can we design companies to be less vulnerable to the demands of capital market actors who operate at a remove from the long-term consequences of business decisions?

- ◆ Can we embrace decision rules that balance short-, medium-, and long-term focus; that prioritize the needs of real investors over traders, respect the constraints of natural resources, and treat employees as an asset rather than a cost?

- ◆ Can we rethink the incentives and decision rules that govern behavior?

The demand for new measures of business success is heard from Main Street to Wall Street. The new rules of the road are already engaged and are anchored in changes taking place in executive suites, boardrooms, classrooms, and employee networks.

What is needed now is to pick up the pace of change.

Values we take for granted in private, founder-led or family firms with consumer brands like Eileen Fisher, Patagonia, and S. C. Johnson are also finding footing in massive, globe-hopping, publicly traded firms. We see the effect of fresh thinking in the bold move by CVS to stop selling cigarettes, in Pepsi and Coke's decision to drop its membership in the plastics industry association and rethink packaging, in Google's pledge to pay a minimum of $15 per hour to contract laborers, and in Shell's decision to quit the US oil lobby and join a growing number of companies committed to aggressive reductions in their carbon footprint.

In each case, we are invited to go deeper, to better understand the motivations and the business model that sit behind the actions—to ensure that these claims and goals signal fundamental change rather than examples of greenwashing. Yet in each example we also see the impact of external and internal forces driving the change and observe a shift in attitudes at the helm.

The forces of change behind the new rules are compelling. They call on our most basic human instincts and align with growing understanding of our dependence on healthy ecosystems and communities. These stories reveal new forms of accountability and inspire fresh thinking about the role and purpose of business. They clarify what is needed now.

In chapter 3, we explore Rule #3 and how actors like Jason Clay of the World Wildlife Fund (WWF) and his peers at Oxfam and Greenpeace employ social media and mine the connections in supply chains to radically redefine and expand the responsibilities—and potential—of brands. In chapter 4, which is concerned with Rule #4, we delve into how the same tools are deployed by employees, inspired by #MeToo, #GoogleWalkout, and #BlackLivesMatter, to give fresh voice to business risk, expand the horizons of business leaders, and rethink the relationship between business and its workers.

Chapter 5, which addresses Rule #5, focuses on financial capital—and how the reality that capital is abundant, not scarce, is reshaping the culture of firms.

New norms of behavior explored in these chapters are evident in newly capitalized companies and are propelled by social networks that link employees with environmental activists and worker organizations. The new rules of engagement challenge the centricity of financial capital and the dominance of public capital markets.

We see the new rules in questions about capital allocation and the "talent strategy" in the executive suite. We can see the change in the 2019 decision of the Business Roundtable—a CEO-only member organization representing many of the largest American companies, the voice of big business and industry in Washington—to rewrite its own mission statement to better reflect the aspirations of many US business leaders. The new rules support the 2020 manifesto on regenerative capitalism declared at the World Economic Forum in Davos. They will help set priorities as we weather and eventually emerge from the COVID-19 crisis and, at last, step into the challenge of addressing the structural underpinnings of both racial inequality and climate change. And, importantly, new definitions of business success have already begun to crack mainstream business classrooms where the story of shareholder primacy began and is still in force—classrooms that orient the analysts at Goldman Sachs and Morgan Stanley and the new recruits at McKinsey and BCG and Deloitte.

The new rules influence—and are influenced by—the change agents who operate within business or challenge it from the outside. They offer a response to withering critiques of capitalism and the decline in trust in business as an institution. The endgame is to secure the remarkable capacity of business to move the needle on socially and environmentally critical goals.

Nitin Nohria writes about leadership. On becoming dean of Harvard Business School, he wrote about the importance of the business sector and private initiative to make any real headway on our most consequential problems—from environmental sustainability and climate change to poverty and fixing the health care system.

When business hangs back, we lose our core capacity to invest in our future. Disheartening examples of business on the sidelines include the failure of business trade groups to organize around a coherent policy on climate change and the choice of many public companies to spend the 2018 tax cuts on share buybacks rather than investing in our economic futures, through the workforce and infrastructure.

What will need to be true to harness business capacity for the work of the world? The interplay of citizen- and employee-activists; unusual leaders; and business-led, socially useful innovations is the juggernaut of change and helps us understand how change takes root and grows. What's needed now is to pick up the pace of change that new rules enable—to separate *real value* from ephemeral, backward-looking measures of financial value.

And importantly, when the system itself is a risk, when markets are on the path to extinction, we see that value creation requires collaboration and co-creation to stabilize conditions, expose the source of the problem, and redesign the business model.

Chapter 6 explores Rule #6, which is about the path to co-creation, the practices and protocols and playbook that ultimately raise the bar across an industry and assure widespread adoption of new business models. Sometimes the chief architect is the brand with the largest exposure to threat. Often, the change requires a trusted broker from outside industry, a curated coalition of like-minded producers, and a client or customer willing—or forced by necessity—to take a long-term view and work to align the market with the limits of growth and new definitions of value.

I hope this book helps business leaders—but also NGOs and foundations—to think deeply about their role as change agents and how critical these new rules are to the future of business and sustainable markets. I hope it illuminates the old norms and governing rules that hold them back. I hope the book strikes a chord with individuals who seek change but are still focusing on rearranging the deck chairs rather than setting an entirely new course of action. I hope the stories make the change visible and accessible—and help put the old rules of value extraction out to pasture. I hope the story of change demonstrates what is possible now.

Decades of work by scholars and campaigners and like-minded business leaders are paying off. The new rules now need air, voice, scholarship, and practice. In chapters 7 and 8, we look at the road ahead, and how the new rules especially need to be seen and understood by the old rule enforcers—strategy firms and investment banks and compensation consultants and accountants and scholars who keep the status-quo-enhancing decision rules alive.

In chapter 7, we take a closer look at *systems design*, especially the role of incentives and rewards for executives. The massive shift toward equity-based pay that began in the 1980s produced runaway CEO pay and a premium for stockholders at the cost of employees and long-term investment; it sends signals that directly undermine the new rules and the urgent call to CEOs to lead on issues of consequence for both business and society. The CEO matters; how she thinks, or what he values, are a critically important starting point for change. We need to redesign pay to catch up with the intentions of executives to serve society.

In the last chapter, we return to the role of teachers in business schools who are catching up in important ways and unleashing new talent—but there is more to do. We especially need to crack the finance classrooms that keep the medieval ways of shareholder-centric thinking in place and reinforce the old story. They respond to the recruiters from financial and other professional services that are still tightening the screws to old specs. As Thomas Berry says, the Old Story is not functioning properly, and we have not learned the New Story.

Enterprises that operate in the give and take of global markets have the power to translate small changes into influential, industry-scale protocols. In incremental but important acts, through the power of small but influential groups that are embracing co-creation over race-to-the-bottom competition, we have begun to see a shift in what constitutes a high-quality business decision that stands the test of time.

The new rules are already written. The forcing mechanisms described in this book and summarized in the chart that follows this introduction give them staying power. Change agents both outside and inside the enterprise are rethinking protocols and decision rules for investment and business strategy.

It's time to play by the new set of rules.

NEW RULES: REAL VALUE

Six New Rules	OLD Rule	Forcing Function: Instruments of Change	NEW Rule—Driver(s) of Real Value Creation
RULE #1 *Reputation, Trust, and Other Intangibles Drive Business Value*	**OLD Rule: Hard assets determine firm value.** Value today is equal to a discount of the future value of fixed assets and predictable cash flows; both decline in value over time.	**Drivers of Change** The balance sheet fails to capture the most important assets: talent, reputation, and key relationships. Risks embedded in the supply chain from human rights to climate change defy conventions of financial valuation and concern host communities, employees, and investors.	**NEW Rule: Reputation, trust, and other intangibles drive business value.** Trust of employees and business partners, premium access to talent, natural resources are the sources of real value and cannot be discounted or measured in traditional ways; to understand their value requires breaking down the walls between the health of the business and the health of the business ecosystem.
RULE #2 *Businesses Serve Many Objectives beyond Shareholder Value*	**OLD Rule: "Shareholder value" or "profit maximization" is the organizing principle of the corporation.** A single objective function—profit—is easy to measure and enables comparisons across divisions or firms. Shareholder value, and its corollary, profit maximization, are the keys to accountability.	**Drivers of Change** Short-term manifestations of fixation with shareholder returns, including earnings management, share buybacks, and outsourcing of jobs, lead to stagnant wages, bad business decisions, and a decline in trust (Enron to Boeing); protests for social and economic justice, from #Occupy to #BlackLivesMatter, disrupt business as usual; executives condemn short-termism and shareholder-centric thinking (even as supporting practices persist).	**NEW Rule: Businesses serve many objectives beyond shareholder value.** The duty of directors is to the health of the enterprise—and thus to the most important contributors of real value. The corporation chooses its purpose; purpose is also revealed through how the company operates and the decisions it makes.
RULE #3 *Corporate Responsibility Is Defined Far outside the Business Gates*	**OLD Rule: Corporate responsibility is defined by host communities and fence-line neighbors.** A corporation has a social responsibility to create jobs, support local services and civic institutions, and contain pollution.	**Drivers of Change** NGOs force change through focus on global brands in an era of radical transparency; public concern about climate change and biodiversity redefines boundaries of responsibility.	**NEW Rule: Corporate Responsibility is defined far outside the business gates.** Corporate responsibility is a moving target: it extends through the supply chain and ecosystem, and even to the private use of products. Governments, NGOs, and an engaged public define the rules of engagement.

RULE #4 *Employees Give Voice to Risk and Competitive Advantage*	**OLD Rule: Labor is a cost to be minimized.** Unions and employee activism drive up costs and impede management from doing its job.	**Drivers of Change** Networked employees and social media; #MeToo, growing inequality, #BlackLivesMatter, and social unrest upset the power balance in companies. Employees connect social and environmental issues to business priorities; they hold the firm accountable in new ways.	**NEW Rule: Employees give voice to risk and competitive advantage.** Employees are business allies in a changing world; they identify future risks and see business opportunity embedded in new norms around sustainability and social responsibility.
RULE #5 *Culture Is King and Talent Rules*	**OLD Rule: Capital is king; shareholders rule.** Financial capital is a scarce resource in a hard-asset world; the company is accountable to the shareholders, who "own" the company.	**Drivers of Change** New business models of the service economy and Internet of Things, low-capital needs, and outsourced labor diminish the power of financial capital and capital markets; values emerge from within; and competition for talent and a focus on innovation and the human element take precedence where capital markets once held sway.	**NEW Rule: Culture is king; talent rules.** Value creation emerges from the culture of the enterprise. The CEO embraces diverse talent and teamwork and focuses on key relationships; competitive advantage is attained through superior customer service, human-centered design, and business models in sync with planetary limits.
RULE #6 *Co-Create to Win*	**OLD Rule: Compete to win.** Competition drives innovation and growth.	**Drivers of Change** Global challenges—climate, inequality, data privacy, species decline—rebound to business and require rapid changes in industry protocols and the competitive landscape to achieve systemic change. NGOs recruit change agents and build successful coalitions to achieve results and raise the bar in industry.	**NEW Rule: Co-create to win.** When the system itself is at risk, real value creation requires enlisting business partners along the supply chain; both NGOs and competitors with aligned interests become business allies.

◆ OLD RULE ◆

Hard assets determine firm value.

Value today is equal to a discount of the future
value of fixed assets and cash flows.

◆ NEW RULE ◆

Reputation, trust, and other intangibles drive business value.

Trust of employees and business partners, and premium access to
talent and natural resources, are the source of real value and cannot
be discounted or measured in traditional ways. To understand
their value requires *breaking down the walls between the health
of the business and the health of the business ecosystem.*

CHAPTER ONE

Rethinking Risk

RULE #1

Reputation, Trust, and Other Intangibles Drive Business Value

To create a fairer economy, one where prosperity is more broadly shared and is therefore more sustainable, we need to reinvigorate a serious discussion about the nature and origin of value.
—MARIANA MAZZUCATO, *THE VALUE OF EVERYTHING*

ON A WARM SEPTEMBER AFTERNOON under a brilliant blue sky, a group of finance scholars were fighting to hear one another over the sound of the Roaring Fork River where it winds through the campus of Aspen Institute in Colorado. It was 2010. The meltdown in the financial markets—from the failures of Bear Stearns and Lehman Brothers to the bailout of major banks—was still reverberating on Wall Street, but especially on Main Street where the value of homes plummeted and the real effects were still felt a decade later.

The purpose of the gathering was to consider what role the finance academy might have played in the turmoil that roiled the markets and defined the early days of a new presidency. Nineteen faculty members drawn from influential business schools—Stanford, NYU, Wharton, the University of Chicago, and Darden at the University of Virginia among them—had accepted our invitation to dialogue. What had we learned—and what were the consequences for how finance is taught?

David Blood had left a leadership position in asset management at Goldman Sachs in 2005 to start a new company called Generation Investment Management. David waved his hand at the rushing stream that tumbled 15 feet below on its journey to the Colorado River and asked the scholars a provocative question: "How do you put a price on the fish?" One of the scholars took the bait: "You can't," he said definitively. It was clear from his quick dismissal of the idea that he thought, "What's more, you *shouldn't.*"

Trying to value the fish in the stream—or the water we drink and the air we breathe—is an abstraction. Yet as we pull back from the river and consider the consequences of an ecosystem at risk, it becomes more than an academic exercise on a warm afternoon in the Rockies. As we consider the livelihoods of communities and quality of life for future generations, we experience challenging questions and very real costs, albeit largely unmeasurable by the traditional tools of finance.

Economists and their colleagues in finance use the label *externality* for a cost imposed on a third party who isn't part of the transaction. In business terms, this might mean the cost of a decision made *inside* the gate on the community that resides outside the gate—for example, the unintended consequence of a product with observable social ramifications, such as the public health costs of alcohol abuse or soda consumption; or how work, structured for maximum efficiency, affects home life or commitment to education. Externalities, by and large, are viewed as a distraction by managers committed to profits and growth.

Social and environmental impacts of business decisions sit outside the frame of financial analysis—until they don't. When we step away from the classroom and observe the world that students enter upon graduation, the need for change in how we invest and how we measure value becomes clear.

Risk analysis is bending to embrace the full life cycle of products. It connects us with the effects of business decisions over time—and is widening in scope to include perspectives of those who help create the product or who feel its effects downstream. Both shape our definitions of value.

These ideas are hardly new. The contemporary framework of the *circular economy*, given visibility by the Ellen MacArthur Foundation and a score of aligned thinkers, has traditional roots; it is part of a conversation about value creation and what to measure and how to measure it that has been evolving since the time of Adam Smith. The idea of thinking in systems echoes a core principle of the Iroquois Confederacy formed by five Native American tribes over 500 years ago. The name of the eco-friendly consumer products company Seventh Generation recalls the Native American ideal of considering the impact of decisions today on generations far into the future. The thesis behind David Blood's successful investment company Generation Investment Management draws from the same philosophy, translating business norms and impact on living systems into investment theory and analysis.

Lorraine Smith, a creative thinker and gifted adviser to our work at the Aspen Institute, weaves together the worlds of business and finance to put nature at the center of the bull's-eye. Maybe because of her Canadian roots, she gets away with questions like "What if the Colorado River were the board of directors—what if the fish owned the business?"

Welcome to the front lines of business, where the game of finance is changing in real time.

Teachers and scholars in management schools are insulated from the pace and chaos of markets and business decision-making. Their job is to observe, interpret the data, and build knowledge, which requires some distance from the day-to-day. In their search for clear decision rules for managers and investors working across a range of industries, they employ both large data sets and case studies.

The tension between theory and practice can be a healthy one. The principal ideas and analytical frameworks that are taught in finance classrooms—and shape the attitudes and frameworks in professional domains like consulting and finance—may lag behind what's current today, the thinking goes, but they stand the test of time.

But what do financial analysts and scholars in finance do when the key assets of the enterprise are unmeasurable?

The simple frameworks that dominated business classrooms in the decades leading up to the turmoil of 2008 were the last gasp of a world ring-fenced by rules about capital formation and valuation. They fail to make the most obvious connections between the real long-term health of the underlying corporation and that of the society and natural systems on which the enterprise depends.

A WAKE-UP CALL IN FINANCE

An early-warning signal of the need for fundamental change emerged early in 2007, in a boom market, before the 2008 collapse. Texas Power & Light, then known as TXU, was one of the most profitable utilities in the country, its growth and prosperity a mirror of the economy of Texas. When the influential private equity firm Kohlberg Kravis Roberts & Co. and its partners, Texas Pacific Group and Goldman Sachs, prepared to take the publicly listed company private, they offered a window into the failure of the old rules of valuation. TXU became a Yale School of Management case study of the need for risk assessment to adjust to new realities and the influence of new voices equipped to go head-to-head with Wall Street.

The deal was ultimately consummated at a valuation of $44 billion—the largest leveraged buyout recorded at the time. Valuations are part art, part mathematics. They are derived from estimates of the market value of current assets of the company plus projections of future asset values, profits, and cash flows—all of which must be stress tested against the competitive environment and future risks to the business model, then discounted back to the value in today's dollars. Citibank, Morgan Stanley, JPMorgan, and others led the placement, and virtually every asset manager and investor of scale on Wall Street, and, by extension, every pension fund in the country, contributed capital—hungry for high-yielding junk bonds at a time of relatively low interest rates.

But that's only part of the story. At the most crucial moment, with the required capital fully subscribed and syndicated and the fees all but booked, the architects of the transaction returned to the drawing board—forced by a network of environmental activists to reexamine assumptions about the future of coal in the state of Texas.

In time, a more environmentally friendly deal went forward, but the wall that insulates the valuation and investment game on Wall Street from the real consequences of investment decisions had begun to crumble. Assumptions about business in the volatile energy sector have continued to morph. We have come to understand brand and business risk in new ways.

We are no longer taken by surprise when B-to-C brands are hijacked by dogged activists determined to make the real costs of operations and the so-called externalities material. What was once outside the scope of the interests of profit-seeking investors blurs the lines between tangible and intangible; the contributors to real value are being redefined, and the central theorem of value is being shaped by critical thinking about the material relationships between and among firm value, human systems, and the biosphere. The simplicity of the single-objective function of maximum profit is no longer deemed superior—or useful.

Within five years after the deal closed, TXU was in shambles and headed toward bankruptcy; the expected cash flow needed to retire massive levels of debt had been undermined by the shift from coal to cheap natural gas. Along the way, TXU was renamed Energy Future Holdings, perhaps in the hope of a better future, and the game started anew.

Welcome to Finance 2020, where pension funds, state controllers, institutional investors, and even the investors' investment bankers have begun to redefine real value and seek a more complex—and useful—understanding of risk.

TXU and the Future of Financial Analysis

In February 2007, at the 11th hour—with the deal doers and bankers and debt syndicators and their clients poised to commit funds for the leveraged buyout of TXU, the Texas utility—a group of scrappy, determined environmental campaigners shot a gaping hole through the spreadsheets, blowing apart the core assumption that another 11 carbon-emitting coal-fired plants would be built to supply energy to the fastest-growing state in the union.

The campaign to thwart the utility's plans began much earlier. As the intention of leading private equity firms to purchase TXU became public in the spring of 2006, a network of local and national environmentalists moved from direct engagement with company executives to a ground game of building public opposition through every means available, from TV ads to swamping the state legislature with letters and petitions. By February 2007, the deal was on ice. When it reemerged a month later, the projected debt was still staggering, but assumptions about the source of energy for the citizens of Texas had changed dramatically. The number of proposed coal-fired power plants had been reduced from 11 to three—a massive scaling back of the utility's plans and a signal of things to come. A number of critics thought even three new carbon-emitting plants was too many; the head of the Rainforest Action Network commented that if the utility was really serious about climate change, it would not build any new coal plants, a sign of further challenges ahead.

The managers of the largest leveraged buyout in history had missed an obvious and tangible risk, leaving egg on the faces of the titans of Wall Street. It was what an investor would consider a *material* risk—one that could produce losses due to a failure to perform under contract.

Ultimately, the chief architects of the campaign against TXU, the Environmental Defense Fund and Natural Resources Defense Council and its affiliates and partners in Texas, backed up by at least some regulators and opinion makers, dropped multiple lawsuits brought against the utility. In exchange, TXU agreed to cancel plans for eight planned coal-fired power plants in Texas and several more in Pennsylvania and Virginia. TXU also agreed to support federal cap-and-trade legislation to regulate CO_2 emissions and to invest $400 million in conservation and energy efficiency.

SIGNS OF CHANGE IN ASSET MANAGEMENT

Thomas Kamei, an investor focused on the Internet sector for Morgan Stanley Investment Management's Counterpoint Global fund, is a member of the Aspen Institute's First Movers Fellowship class of 2015. First Movers meet in cohorts of 21 fellows per class to hone skills and build their know-how about creating change from within companies. The fellows are drawn from every corner of the business world—from heavy equipment manufacturers to consumer products, finance to retail. They are selected for their commitment to the complex task of aligning business decisions with the long-term health of society—a complicated endeavor that depends on new business models and metrics.

Thomas was born to investment. At age 10, he began an annual pilgrimage with his mother to sit at the feet of the Oracle of Omaha, Warren Buffett. In 2019, he and his colleagues at Morgan Stanley Investment Management began to test a model for assessing risk that Thomas started working on during his fellowship year. The model offers a clear-eyed view of both risk and rewards when the rules no longer support walls between business and society. Long-term investing demanded a fresh approach, and Thomas was offered the chance to experiment.

The fund that employs Thomas Kamei seeks superior long-term returns for patient investors. Counterpoint Global is designed to identify and invest in undervalued stocks for the long term. Counterpoint is one of the most successful long-only funds in the market, and Thomas's job was to study companies and understand risks and opportunities now and into the future in order to pick stocks that have a long-term competitive advantage.

With a doggedness that is both admirable and the key to systemic change, Thomas has helped widen the lens at Counterpoint Global to consider material, yet difficult-to-measure, disruptions from unusual places. In one example, Thomas and his colleagues aligned with Lonely Whale, an NGO working on eliminating plastics in oceans, to engage

Starbucks on the use of plastic straws. Thomas considered Starbucks's iconic green straw for frozen drinks a "gateway plastic"—not by any measure the key to protecting ocean ecology yet an obvious target for campaigners seeking massive change in norms around producer responsibility. Following a series of conversations in 2018 highlighting the material risks of inaction around plastic waste, CEO Howard Schultz responded to the call from his early and important investor Counterpoint Global and put a process in motion to eliminate the straw. By the end of 2019, Pepsi and Coke had announced the decision to drop out of the Plastics Industry Association and to double down on investment in alternatives to plastics in packaging.

As Morgan Stanley's Counterpoint Global fund began to test Thomas's framework, it became not only an analytical tool but also a guide to engagement with company management. The framework features a dashboard of data and a series of questions designed to unlock the attitudes, embedded incentives, and *mindset* of the target enterprise.

The quantitative measures on the analyst's dashboard help provide insight into a company's alignment with long-term value creation. The methodology that Thomas scoped out and continues to develop employs questions to take the measure of leadership and commitment—what Thomas calls *agency*. Do the executives have the bearing and aligned incentives to take a long-term view? Is the culture equipped to understand the collision of changing expectations among investors and the shifts in social norms and environmental trends that are on the horizon—and that could rebound to the firm? Is management awake to the opportunity that the trends present, as well as the risk?

This kind of thoughtful analysis requires more than a simple spreadsheet.

Thomas and his colleagues at Counterpoint Global are dealing in real time with the limitations of the decision rules taught in finance classrooms everywhere. The discounted cash flow (DCF) model has glaring shortcomings.

First, DCF fails to capture material, but hard-to-measure, risks—such as a sudden shift in consumer attitudes toward plastic bottles or consumption of meat, or a sustained drought deep in the supply chain, or a potential strike or employee protest. In fact, material risks—the kind that blow a hole in the spreadsheet—may not show up at all. And the disruptions that do show up may require such a long-term view—from the impact of climate change to trends in labor markets and debates about a livable wage—as to disappear through deep discounting of future costs.

And second, the future opportunity embedded in risks may be hidden from the business managers buried in the need to report in 90-day increments to conventional analysts who consider "long term" to be three to five years, or even one year—far less than a normal business cycle. The fact that most asset managers are on a yearly bonus cycle based on recent stock performance compounds the problem.

The kind of analysis and direct engagement that Thomas and his colleagues employ works best with a highly curated portfolio of dozens of companies. It's kind of like hand-to-hand combat: you can look the target in the eye and assess their readiness for battle. Risk management at an index fund with thousands of stocks in the portfolio, or a large mutual fund with hundreds of investments, requires a different approach.

For example, BlackRock, with $7 *trillion* in assets under management, is the largest investor in the world and a significant force in both public and private markets. When the CEO of BlackRock speaks out, he is heard in the C-suite of every publicly traded company. Larry Fink's annual letter to CEOs in 2020 cited the Sustainability Accounting Standards Board (SASB) as a useful, comprehensive reporting framework. SASB experienced a fivefold increase in the number of daily downloads in the two weeks following the publication of Larry's letter. And even more important for SASB is that the new visitors to their site included more business managers inside corporate accounting, risk management, and the legal department.

Yet, managing to the rapidly changing expectations of the ultimate investor is nothing if not complex. So-called ESG investing—short for environment, social, and governance investment objectives—embraces a crazy quilt of issues du jour. Managers of ESG funds, like all asset managers, compete for clientele and are measured by growth in assets under management. The competitive environment produces a confusing array of individual funds marketed as gun-free or pro-diversity to attract investors who want to match their values and pocketbook—but without sacrificing returns or the safety of holding a truly broad index of stocks, like the S&P 500.

The growing array of investment products may be a positive trend and signaling device to corporations—but it can also be confusing, or not what it appears to be. Matt Levine, the voice behind the popular and often hilarious Bloomberg column "Money Stuff," calls the natural desire of ESG fund managers to exclude as few stocks as possible "grading on the curve."

If ESG investments are designed to keep investors happy—i.e., take a stand without incurring much risk—can they actually drive behavior change in companies? How does an asset manager assess worker-friendliness or compare the track records of different companies on human rights deep in supply chains? What measures of carbon output work best across multiple industries without losing the plot? And which is more important as an investment strategy: modest but measurable change across Pepsi's massive supply chain, or supporting a start-up or small private company with superior standards?

Setting the rules of engagement in the C-suite is a complicated endeavor. The backward-looking metrics and algorithms behind the marketing of eco- or worker-friendly portfolios fail to capture the complexity of managing sensibly with the goal of real, long-term value creation.

What is required now to keep pace with public expectations for risk assessment and valuation in a changing world?

In September 2019, on the stage of *Fortune*'s Global Sustainability Forum in Yunnan, China, Dutch designer Daan Roosegaarde had this to say about the planetary limits we face, which have seized the attention of both individual investors and those who manage their money:

> Don't be afraid, be curious. I don't believe in utopia, I believe in *protopia*: designing prototypes for solutions that create a better world and that can be realized. As humans, we learn, we fail, and we evolve. Stop whining and worrying. We need to fix it.[1]

Today, a robust industry of committed analysts and consultants is trying to do just that, inspired by the pioneering work of architect Bill McDonough; Arie de Geus of Royal Dutch Shell; Paul Hawken, founder of Smith & Hawken; Marjorie Kelly, author of *Owning Our Future*; and others who design business models that work with natural systems and hold out *regeneration* of life-sustaining natural systems as the goal.

Sustainability experts work with business executives to understand, and price, the real costs of industrial processes—and to execute the changes needed to establish a new baseline for corporate performance. The first step is what one innovative business association, Future-Fit, calls "break even" goals. But companies able to capture both the best talent and the best press today go further; they move beyond a do-no-harm mindset.

Leading companies design products and industrial processes within the limits of natural resources. Levi Strauss's founding story began in the Gold Rush. It links innovative design with community values and continues to draw talent committed to both high labor standards and resource conservation. Bart Sights is one of five Aspen First Mover Fellows who hail from Levi Strauss. Bart grew up in the textiles business in Henderson, Kentucky, where his family's denim operation had Levi Strauss as a customer. When denim production moved offshore, Levi Strauss recruited Bart to support their manufacturing operations, first in Turkey and then at the San Francisco headquarters, where Bart runs the company's Eureka Innovation Lab. In his fellowship year, Bart tested the use of lasers to replace chemicals in the production of "distressed" jeans. The process has raised the bar in the textile industry and continues Levi Strauss's tradition of incorporating environmental values in design.

Dow Chemical's decade-long partnership with the Nature Conservancy brought the engineers in close collaboration with the environmentalists to restore the wetlands downstream from Dow's facilities. Microsoft's commitment announced in early 2020 to recapture by 2050 all of the carbon released directly by the company and its electricity usage *since it was founded* will require technology not yet fully at scale. A $1 billion Climate Innovation Fund established by the company will become a resource for others; it recognizes that to solve our planet's carbon issues will require technology that does not yet exist.

How do these companies capture the benefit of these innovations? Surveys that measure employee engagement or consumer attitudes, such as net promoter scores, help inform business decisions, but the benefit to the company may not be tangible enough to show up in ticks in the stock price or in profitability today. After all, the primary motivation for discrete investments by these companies—Levi Strauss, Dow Chemical, and Microsoft—is aimed at the health of the ecosystem—not the business bottom line. These executives are acting on instinct; they believe in a tangible payback if they do the right thing today. The idea that externalities may simply be ignored in asset allocation and investment is getting harder to fathom.

Chris McKnett of Wells Fargo and Ashley Schulten of BlackRock are also Aspen Fellows. Chris has built a career in finance around making "ESG values" tangible. In a compelling TED Talk, he translates these ideals as a matter of risk—*and* opportunity.[2] He gives voice to the "woke" asset managers, like Ashley, who value ecologically sound products and more resilient business models. Ashley leads the coordination of ESG integration, climate risk evaluation, and sustainable investing for BlackRock's fixed income division, where she explores innovative approaches to understanding business risks of climate change. She uses climate models to reveal physical, as well as socioeconomic, impacts and a user-friendly interface to map these impacts against financial asset valuations.

Ashley wants investors to connect the dots between a changing climate and management reality; for example, if company assets are likely to flood, do financial models capture the risk? By helping institutions—pensions, endowments, and mutual funds—manage long-term risk, she links investment to business decisions and makes the executive's job easier, not harder. In turn, Ashley's work is aligned with the almost infinite time horizons of the vast majority of individual savers and equity investors—those saving long term for college or retirement.

Ashley, Thomas, Chris, and their peers throughout the finance industry defy conventional ways of assessing risk. They also stand against short-term market pressures from investors who have little interest in the longer-term prospects of the enterprise but who influence norms and decision rules in both public and private markets.

Take, for example, the world of private equity, an elite and fast-growing corner of investment where "qualified" investors—high net worth individuals and institutions—seek higher yields beyond the intense scrutiny and regulation of the public markets.

Private equity firms like KKR and Texas Pacific Group, the partners in the TXU deal, have a modest investment horizon for the companies they acquire, typically five to seven years, long enough to upgrade technology and make other changes in strategy and management with an eye to greater efficiency, productivity, and return on investment (ROI). Greater productivity typically requires selling off parts of the business and reducing head count. Most private equity deals carry heavy debt loads to finance the purchase and subsequent investments. The financial gains are captured when the company is sold back to the public market or to another private investor at a higher valuation.

Critics like economist Mariana Mazzucato turn our assumptions about what is productive upside down. In her book *The Value of Everything: Making and Taking in the Global Economy*, Mazzucato revives an old conversation about what constitutes productive work—a debate that threads the entire history of economic thought. Productivity is a measure of output. It was once tied to land and then, in the industrial age, to labor itself. For Adam Smith and those who followed, the activities that help facilitate commerce were considered outside the productive boundary. Activities like finance and investment, and in fact the entire mercantile sector of buying and selling of goods, were not measured as part of the economic output of the country.

Today, productivity has a very different spin. Private equity firms have both admirers and detractors, but both acknowledge that these investment funds measure economic productivity principally through the lens of returns to investors. In recent years, the stories of private investors preying on Main Street to identify the next target and extract profits have become part of the narrative about where the profession of finance has failed us. Examples also originate in the public capital markets where corporate raiders, today's "activist" investors, demand a seat on the board to oversee goals that are short term in nature, to institute measures that "release value"—i.e., raise the stock price for short-term investors. Research calculates the cost of hedge fund activism on long-term stock value—but, more important, for other stakeholders who bear the real costs over time.[3]

Senator Tammy Baldwin, Democrat of Wisconsin, made a case example out of a paper mill forced to capitulate to a private takeover:

> Wausau Paper in Wisconsin . . . had a 100-year history of making paper in Wisconsin. When a wolf pack seized control, they forced out the company's executives and sold several mills—causing one Wisconsin town to declare bankruptcy. The hedge funds demanded that Wausau abandon investments in future growth and instead borrow to buy back shares and boost stock prices. This example is tragic, but not unique; there were 348 activist campaigns in 2014. The number has risen annually by 60 percent since 2010.[4]

The case of Wausau Paper is compelling but complicated. The paper industry is built on a business model of extraction of natural resources—and the purpose of the buyout had nothing to do with enhancing the health and well-being of the people or the ecosystem that sustains life. None of the players who had built or supported the enterprise—neither the employees, nor the towns, nor the local businesses—enjoyed any of the upside of the transaction.

Stories like these may have cost former Massachusetts governor Mitt Romney, who entered politics after a career at Bain Capital, his bid for the presidency in 2012. When Deval Patrick, also a former governor of Massachusetts, threw his hat in the ring for president in 2019, he resigned from his post at Bain and removed the company from his campaign bio.

The tide may have begun to turn, even in the less-than-transparent world of private equity, as wealth concentration escalates and firms have been forced to reckon with new rules of finance—i.e., embedding environmental costs of doing business and balancing returns to investors with jobs and returns to workers. The investment firm Apollo signaled a desire to change the conversation when it rescued Hostess and its iconic brands out of bankruptcy, and then began to experiment with employee profit-sharing as a pathway to better relations with workers and, yes, higher productivity. Leading firms like KKR and Carlyle now employ ESG specialists to alert analysts to the human and environmental costs of business as usual. The conversation in private equity firms has begun to widen from risk mitigation to value creation: by focusing on intangible values, can the firm create a better opportunity and return for the investors, the portfolio company, and society?

Marty Lipton is a founder of the law firm Wachtell, Lipton, Rosen & Katz and inventor of the "poison pill" to thwart unfriendly takeovers. In the article "Takeover Bids in the Target's Boardroom," published in the *Business Lawyer* in 1979, Marty asks if "the long-term interests of the nation's corporate system and economy should be jeopardized in order to benefit speculators interested not in the vitality and continued existence of the business enterprise in which they have bought shares, but only in a quick profit on the sale of those shares."[5]

Beginning in the 1980s and intensifying since, the world of finance in both public and private capital markets has confounded our view of what constitutes good business management. From outside the finance industry, the different kinds of investments tend to confuse more than clarify objectives. What are the goals of the business, and are they aligned or at odds with the goals of different kinds of investors?

Roger Martin is a well-known business strategist and former dean of the Rotman School of Business at the University of Toronto. Martin accepted an invitation to join an Aspen Institute dialogue convened at the close of the go-go stock market years of the 1990s. The design of the meeting enabled the participants to dive into the murky area of the changing role of corporations in society to better understand what is needed to withstand race-to-the bottom market pressures. How might we support the kinds of decisions that create real value for the business and society?

Roger Martin writes about this challenge. In his book *Fixing the Game: Bubbles, Crashes, and What Capitalism Can Learn from the NFL*, he distinguishes between two kinds of market activity. The *real market* includes everything needed to create the goods and services to serve the customer—i.e., R&D, sourcing, manufacturing and production, marketing, and all the labor and infrastructure to support business activity. The *expectations market* is about investing in and betting on the future value of shares of stock—shares that are initially issued to raise cash to support the company's growth but continue to circulate in a secondary market with only an indirect connection to the company. Today's stock price is influenced by myriad events and macroeconomic trends that may have little to do with the fundamentals of the business itself.

To bring home the point, Martin uses the analogy of American football, in which the real market and the expectations market are kept separate. Players on the football field—and the coaching staff and managers and anyone who can *influence* the game—are prohibited from betting on the *outcome* of the game.[6]

In US public companies, managers are expected to tend to both—the market strategy and execution on the one hand, but also the stock price. As we will see in chapter 7, the design of pay compounds the lack of clarity between these aims and resulting tensions between executives rewarded mostly for increases in the stock price and the workers seeking higher pay, benefits, and financial security.

CHANGE IN THE C-SUITE: WHAT MATTERS MOST?

As COVID-19 wreaked havoc in communities and the national and global economy imploded in the early spring of 2020, Eric Motley, an Aspen Institute colleague, wrote an email to the staff of the Institute about the dilemma of decision-making and how abstract ideas and tradeoffs had materialized in this moment—had become "current, real, and disturbing."[7]

Eric quotes Mortimer Adler, an educator and philosopher from the University of Chicago and architect of the Aspen Seminar in the 1950s—still a core offering of the Aspen Institute today. In *How to Read a Book*, Adler wrote, "The essence of tragedy is time, or rather the lack of it. There is no problem in any Greek tragedy that could not have been solved if there had been enough time, but there is never enough. Decisions, choices have to be made in a moment."[8]

Eric ends his message building on the ideas of Jim O'Toole, whose contemporary and powerful contributions to the Aspen Seminar are explored in his book *The Executive's Compass*.[9] Eric writes,

> At best those decision-points are informed by a moral compass, our own internal sense of right and wrong, shaped and sharpened by education and experience. Nonetheless our moral framework, inherent in its very formation, is both complex and often contradictory. At the very intersection of society lies both a tragic and ironic sense of history . . . and both the collision of values and the dialectical dilemma of liberty, equality, efficiency, community. And I would add, equity.

As the pandemic crisis unfolded in spring 2020, the question of *equity* reentered the American conversation. Like other qualities of business culture, equity is hard to measure; it depends on what lens you apply, whose needs you consider. Equity matters little in the pricing of assets, and until recently, equity, or fairness, has not been much of a factor in the allocation of pay and rewards. As a *value* of business culture, equity has an intangible quality to it—yet the absence of equity is deeply felt and is now at the center of discourse in the public square, and within organizations of all kinds.

At this writing, Amazon warehouse and Instacart delivery workers are on the front lines of a massive shift in buying habits under restrictions on public assembly. As jobs melted away under stay-at-home orders, it took courage for these employees providing essential services to protest their working conditions and a lack of protocols to protect worker health. As with the courageous nurses and orderlies caring for patients in hospitals and nursing homes, for the laborers behind commerce, it is a matter of life and death.

In a scene that recalls labor protests of yore, a growing number of workers have found their voice for the first time in a generation. The question of equity is back on the table. Where and how it will be applied is too early to tell.

In this moment, executives are again asked to do more—to move beyond markets to a new way of thinking and assessing value that is critical to both stability and growth. Tierney Remick, who co-chairs the CEO search practice at Korn Ferry and is a member of the advisory board of the Aspen Institute Business and Society Program, says highly effective CEOs are both strong commercial leaders and courageous social architects.

CEOs today require different skills and new ways of managing. They are whiplashed by rapid shifts in the expectations communicated by their own employees and the fast-paced changes at the intersection of business disruption, evolution in technology, and societal expectations. When the response led by the executive is authentic—i.e., when it lives up to its promises—it affects business operations as well as firm reputation. It can be the very key to understanding and building long-term value. Authenticity is evident in the actions of effective leaders but is difficult to measure—and cannot be discounted.

◆ ◆ ◆

Roy Vagelos was CEO of Merck in the 1980s. His closest advisers cautioned against his decision to produce and distribute the drug Mectizan, a cure for a disease known as river blindness, whose victims had no means to pay for the drug. Merck led on private investment in a public good, and Vagelos demonstrated a keen understanding of long-term value creation. We will explore the connections between corporate purpose and his decision in the next chapter.

Doug McMillon, CEO of Walmart, was called to act in the wake of mass shootings in Walmart stores in 2019—one outside of El Paso, and the other south of Memphis in the town of Southaven, Mississippi. In the space of a week, 24 customers and staff were killed. After a period of consultation, McMillon announced that all Walmart stores everywhere would stop selling handguns and ammo, including ammunition for military-style weapons. His decision departed from earlier policy, and in the times and social mosaic of the United States, the implications for the business were uncertain. He had listened to his employees.

With a nod to Theodore Roosevelt, who became president in 1901 after the assassination of William McKinley at a time of growing tension between capital and labor, participants in an Aspen dialogue began to refer to this realm of thinking and acting as *market civitas*. President Roosevelt's battle with the railroads and monopolists had multiple objectives—a "square deal" for citizens, and a different kind of consciousness and civic engagement, not unlike the need for managers to consider a company's social and environmental values and impacts today.

Market civitas, in the new millennium, requires business to lend its considerable weight to the health of the commons: to critical infrastructure, an educated labor force, and equal access for all to public goods. Market civitas requires wise use of consumer data, mitigation of a warming climate, and the end of commodification of nature and our separation from it. To make real progress, business leaders need to lean on their trade associations to advance supportive public policy, including a price on carbon and a fair tax system for future collective benefit.

But market civitas also requires private investment of time and money. An airline invests in technology to reduce carbon emissions; a tech company transforms the rules on data privacy; a clothing manufacturer redefines global protocols for contract labor. As we will explore more fully in chapter 6, sometimes market civitas means engaging in complicated coalitions of change agents and competitors. As Amazon found out when it gave up on its national bid for a second headquarters city, market civitas means taking public benefit as seriously as private benefit.

Market civitas is about both utilizing business soft power and deploying business capacity with wisdom and with respect for the institutions that uphold democracy and community.

The PR firm Edelman produces an annual survey called the Trust Barometer to capture public opinion about institutions: government, business, media, and civil society organizations. In May 2020, as the COVID-19 surge commanded headlines and boardrooms, Edelman did a refresh of the 2020 Trust Barometer released in January; it found an anxious public with renewed trust in government, but also heightened expectations that business could put "people before profits." The interest in business is anchored to perception about business capability—i.e., problem-solving capacity and an ability to put people to work. When government fails us, it is unrealistic to wait—the public wants action now.

Both COVID-19 and the climate crisis put a spotlight on the intersection of the health of business and the health of the society. For the public's confidence in business to be borne out requires business

In Pursuit of Market Civitas

The right moves in the spirit of market civitas can be amorphous or may require a crystal ball. The key to unlocking the playbook in the realm of market civitas is to have a deep understanding of what drives real business value: the business investments and decisions that enable societies to thrive within healthy living systems.

- For a mining operation like De Beers, it means earning the political and community support to operate, for decades to come, in an environmentally sensitive region.

- For PepsiCo and Levi Strauss, it requires deep understanding of water conservation and the long-term health of agriculture and commodities from potatoes to cotton.

- For Starbucks, it requires working with third-party actors—from Oxfam to the United Nations—who know what constitutes fair exchange with the traditional societies who manage and harvest rare varieties of coffee beans.

- For the waste hauler Waste Management, it means taking a very long-term view of the research and development required to create and manage an entirely new waste stream for organic, compostable material with the potential to create value rather than rot in costly landfills.

acumen coupled with emotional intelligence and a keen understanding of the complex interplay of democracy and free markets—of culture and commerce.

THE CHALLENGE FOR FINANCE SCHOLARS WHEN THE KEY ASSETS ARE INTANGIBLE

Finance faculty who teach valuation and investment as a math problem—take the future projected value of hard assets and revenues and discount it against an implied rate of return to determine the value today—are teaching only one tool in a much more complex tool kit required to succeed as a chief executive today, or even as the CFO. Many MBAs in elite schools end up in professions that advise business. They need much more than the decision rules built on classical economic thinking. These students want to make a real difference in how the executive acts.

A business is nothing without a workforce that believes in the product or standing in the community that governs access to tangible assets—clean water, infrastructure, minerals. A business that adds value across the key relationships upon which it depends is an enterprise or brand worth working for and investing in. It is much, much more than a piece of real estate.

As finance faculty wrestle with demands for change in their discipline—what counts the most and what can be discounted—they are swimming in the wake that still swirls around Milton Friedman.

At the end of the 2010 meeting of finance faculty in Aspen mentioned at the beginning of the chapter, a seasoned scholar and teacher at one of the most highly regarded business schools in the country offered up this thought as a place to restart the conversation: "Over the course of a career, my students rotate through jobs on Wall Street, but also through the Treasury Department. I need them to understand the balancing act between private inurement and public benefit. What do I teach in cases where there is misalignment between private gain and public welfare?"

The same can be said of business managers whose license to operate is on the line.

Finance scholars are tough nuts to crack, but real change is occurring in business schools, and within the proximity of the core finance classroom. Michael Porter and George Serafeim from Harvard Business School, and their colleague Mark Kramer, wrote in *Institutional Investor* about the state of finance in 2019 and its aims:

> We believe that the most fundamental purpose of investors is to allocate capital to those businesses that can use it well in meeting society's most important needs at a profit. Without the effective investment of capital in the real economy, society cannot prosper.

But we live in a world today where investors are profiting while much of society is struggling. This disconnect is a threat not only to the legitimacy of capital markets, but also to the future of capitalism itself.[10]

If you scan the dozens of faculty members who have won one of Aspen's Ideas Worth Teaching Awards, very few are in finance. There are courses that have examined exemplary uses of finance and financial tools, such as microcredit, and courses that look at ethical dilemmas in finance or even the failure of the finance system. But the fundamentals of how finance is taught, or might be taught differently today, still seem off-limits or very complicated to unwind.

Anat Admati is on the faculty at Stanford's Graduate School of Business, where she is a professor of finance and economics. After a number of years of exploring different disciplines as a lens on the near-failure of the financial system in 2008, she began to experiment with a course called Finance and Society, which she describes this way in the syllabus:

> This interdisciplinary course will discuss the role of the financial system within the broader economy and the interactions between the financial system and the rest of society. . . . [It will] cover the basic economic principles essential for understanding the role of finance in the economy, and discuss policy issues around financial regulation.

She tackles the financial system, from microfinance to global megabanks and the role of regulation—why needed and how executed. She covers the domain of fiduciary duty, when you are responsible for "other people's money" and the governance issues that result; and she examines what she terms the "politics of banking and finance."

Anat is comfortable in an interdisciplinary environment and encourages students from law and policy to come mix it up with the students at the business school. She recently launched the school's Corporations and Society Initiative to bring the dialogue into the open.

She is eager to explore the disconnect at the heart of the financial meltdown and described her reason for creating the new initiative for a Stanford GSB publication:

> Financial firms can do all the things that we tell them to do to max-imize shareholder value and yet still mess up everything—make reckless mortgage loans, bundle and sell them around the world, and create a fragile system that takes down the global economy when homeowners start defaulting. . . . How can that be? How is that tolerated?
>
> It turns out the rules were bad, and our assumptions about markets were wrong. Worse, as I looked more closely, I encountered false or misleading claims that seemed to support and enable the system. Our teachings and research assume or suggest that if cor-porations maximize shareholder value or stock price, that's good for society. But it turns out you can do considerable harm as you chase these targets.[11]

Anat's curiosity about what went wrong led her into other fields— the social sciences and law—to understand, as Thomas Berry says, the Old Story and the need for a new one: "I started getting a better under-standing and insight in ways that I would not get from the standard models in economics and finance. And I began to question a lot of our basic assumptions."

She mused about a Capitalism 3.0 course that might build a bridge between observing what's wrong and teaching finance differently, and said she was inspired by the vision of Arjay Miller, who served as Stanford GSB dean from 1969 to 1979. Miller created the public man-agement program that first began to host teaching and scholarship on questions of business accountability and, today, the content about social enterprises and nonprofits that deploy capital to good ends.

It's a start.

Rebecca Henderson teaches strategy to MBAs at the Harvard Busi-ness School. She was recently appointed course head for a required leadership curriculum, the seeds of which began as an elective called

Reimagining Capitalism. Her teaching earned an Ideas Worth Teaching Award from the Aspen Institute, and in 2020, she published a book with the same title: *Reimagining Capitalism in a World on Fire*.

The first year, 28 students showed up. The course created significant buzz, and the next year nearly 400 students applied to take it—nearly half of the entire second-year class. The success of the course is testament to a hunger for knowledge about what capitalism can and should deliver—and for know-how about managing between the health of the enterprise and the health of the society on which the enterprise depends.

Rebecca uses a classic 2x2 matrix to lay out the contemporary challenge of managers: the tension between decisions that work best for "me, now" versus the long-term and future needs of "the other." That quadrant labeled "the other" captures complicated questions like business dependency on the host community, complexity in the supply chain, and the costs of resource use on generations in the future. The manager's need to balance multiple perspectives and the dynamic effects of business decisions today is clear and compelling. It is also real to the students who are entering business at a time of remarkable complexity.

This change in business teaching mirrors the changes in investment, where asset managers consider criteria relevant to the needs and hopes of a new generation of investors, for whom the importance of a healthy stream can no longer be ignored.

◆ ◆ ◆

To rewrite the rules of and connect these dots within business begins with a deceptively simple question: What is the purpose of the enterprise?

The purpose of the corporation is not a slogan; it is the key to unlocking the value of intangible assets—to developing and sustaining the trust of consumers, investors, and employees themselves. And as the next chapter makes clear, the *purpose* of the enterprise is best understood, and fully revealed, through the actions of management.

◆ OLD RULE ◆

Shareholder value or profit maximization is the organizing principle of the corporation.

A single objective function—profit—is easy to measure and enables comparisons across divisions or firms. Shareholder value and its corollary, profit maximization, are the keys to accountability.

◆ NEW RULE ◆

Businesses serve many objectives beyond shareholder value.

The primary duty of directors is to attend to the health of the enterprise—and thus to the most important contributors of real value. A corporation chooses its purpose; *purpose is also revealed through how the company operates and the decisions it makes.*

CHAPTER TWO

The Question of Business Purpose

RULE #2

Businesses Serve Many Objectives beyond Shareholder Value

Profits sustain us, but they don't define us.
—MARJORIE SCARDINO, FORMER CEO, PEARSON

KAREN BRENNER teaches Law and Business at New York University. She takes her students through a simple exercise each semester: filing to obtain a license to open a business. It costs $60 and requires you to fill out a form that asks the purpose of the enterprise. It's a teachable moment: *Purpose* is the starting point.

Sadly, the advice typically given by your accountant, should you consult one, is to say that the purpose is whatever the law deems permissible. But the lesson from Karen's classroom still stands. Because you are the principal of the business, it's up to you. *You* decide the ends to which you will deploy the license to operate.

It may feel like parsing words, but the purpose of *business* is not the same as the purpose of the *corporation*. The purpose of a corporation is a legal construct. The purpose of a business goes deeper; it is given meaning by the people who lead and who are employed there, past and present. While the leader's intentions may be defining, they are not static; the business is continually influenced by systems and forces that embrace and shape both the intentions and the execution.

The importance of understanding both the legal framework and what truly animates the business—its purpose—first became clear to me in a conversation with an executive about a decision he made a decade earlier. In 1997, toward the end of my tenure at the Ford Foundation, I spent an hour with Roy Vagelos, who as CEO of the pharmaceutical company Merck gave the go-ahead to produce a drug with no commercial value—but whose properties had incalculable human benefit.

The drug is Mectizan, also known by its generic name, ivermectin. Mectizan is still produced by Merck today as a money-losing but effective prevention and treatment for river blindness, a disease spread by infected blackflies in breeding grounds near fast-moving rivers and streams in remote regions throughout sub-Saharan Africa. It is also found in discrete locations in Latin America and Yemen.

A Harvard Business School case chronicles the decision that Vagelos faced: whether the company should engage in public health activities when the costs of success have no bounds, and the benefits to the company are, at best, intangible. River blindness is a devastating but curable condition. What is the right thing to do when you learn that your intellectual property could bring renewed life and hope to the victims but no revenues to support its production?

When appeals by Vagelos to everyone from the UN to the White House failed to identify a public entity willing to take the patent off his hands and produce and administer the drug, he decided that Merck would forge ahead.

The company's investment in 1988, backed by Vagelos's commitment to produce the drug "free of cost for as long as needed, as much as needed, and wherever needed" is indeed a great case for the classroom; it's a leadership story and ethical dilemma. But it's more than that. The Merck case became a compelling example of long-term thinking—and a window into what makes a company tick.

For Merck to succeed in this venture required complex partnerships that connected the science, drug production, and remote villages in infected areas. A network of public health agents and protocols was needed to turn drug delivery into sustained practice. The gambit is paying off on the ground, as onchocerciasis—river blindness—is gradually being eradicated in areas where these practices have been effective.

Decades after Vagelos made his move, Jim Yong Kim, president of the World Bank Group, declared Merck's steadfast decision to produce and distribute the drug until the disease was eradicated a "game-changing intervention." It also produced meaningful benefits for Merck that are difficult to capture on the balance sheet.

The CEO's decision was ultimately viewed as a public relations coup and a defining moment for a company dedicated to human health, but Vagelos first had to overcome resistance within his own ranks. His executive team rightly feared the slippery slope of engagement in a campaign with no end in sight. Yes, they could create some goodwill, but it would be offset by an extended liability.

In my interview with Vagelos, he spoke about the MBA classes that he had visited for years after the case was produced—and how even with the gift of hindsight, students would question his course of action and recommend against it. Vagelos spoke about other moments in Merck's history that he had learned from and that had set the stage for his decision. After the end of World War II, during the transition of occupied Japan to self-governance, Merck helped Japan develop its own capability for drug manufacturing. Similar investments in a developing China had positioned the company as a valued development and trade partner.

Yet, what had truly unlocked the Mectizan decision for Vagelos?

"We are nothing," he said, "without the scientists who are the creative force behind drug discovery. What message would it send to our employees if we decided against manufacturing a drug that cures a disease as devastating as river blindness?"

It could have turned out differently.

Vagelos was the CEO but he was first and foremost a scientist. He was crystal clear about what makes Merck tick. He understood the foundation of the company's long-term success, that access to scientific talent is the scarce resource that distinguishes the brand—and that enables the company to fulfill its mission to "discover, develop and provide innovative products and services that save and improve lives around the world."

The hour I spent with him—his demeanor, his clarity about the importance of science and drug discovery, his *humanness*—is still with me over two decades later. The values he lived by and his keen understanding of the company he inherited are what enabled him to become a great leader.

Fast-forward to today's culture of shareholder value. What is the purpose of Valeant?

In 2015, Valeant was a hot stock. Like Merck, Valeant was considered a drug company, but it did not engage in drug discovery or create its own IP. The company's revenues came from buying other drug companies, stripping out costs, and aggressively pricing the products on the shelves, even pushing product through pharmacies that the company controlled. The organizing principle was sharholder value maximization. Aggressive stock targets were embedded in the compensation plan.

Where does the patient fit into this business model? Who is drawn to work at this company? Access to medicines for those in need does not appear to enter into the equation. In fact, it's impossible to classify the company and how it made money as within the bounds of productive activity, in an economic sense.

By the close of 2015, Valeant's operating model was falling apart, and the stock price had imploded. The organizing principle of shareholder value, or share price maximization, had reached its natural limit.

Sometimes, writing the company's purpose is merely a PR exercise. It's easy to be cynical when companies coin statements lofty enough to serve as fodder for late-night comedians. Casper, the mattress company, became the butt of jokes for this slogan: "Awakening the potential of a well-rested world." Adam Neumann, cofounder of WeWork, I believe actually thought he was in business to "elevate the world's consciousness." His quest will be remembered as a red flag more than an inspiration to either workers or customers.

WeWork may have been poorly managed, but the company provides a useful service to individuals, entrepreneurs, and even large corporations that are seeking more flexible ways to house employees. Clarity of purpose, anchored into the business model, could have been a useful foundation for decision-making—an organizing principle for how to allocate both investment capital and talent.

The true purpose of the enterprise is more than words on a page. It signals intentions and understanding of the context of the business. But here's the bottom line: in all companies, *purpose is also revealed.*

Valeant lived by profit maximization, while the CEO of Merck lived by his keen understanding of science and the importance of the scientist as the doorway to drug discovery and delivering value to patients.

As mentioned in chapter 1, BlackRock CEO Larry Fink writes annual letters to the CEOs of public companies. With its $7 trillion under management, BlackRock is the single largest investor in most stocks. In 2018, Fink called for each CEO to consider his or her company's purpose. He asked the executive to take a fresh look at why the public offers the business a license to operate with its specific protections and benefits.

Larry wrote, "Purpose is not a mere tagline or marketing campaign; it is a company's fundamental reason for being—what it does every day to create value for its stakeholders. Purpose is not the sole pursuit of profits but the animating force for achieving them."

PURPOSE REVEALED

The process of drug discovery is a long and complicated one and requires a commitment to science, a high degree of professional standards and protocols, flawless execution against operating goals, and a keen sense of the public license to operate. If you become CEO of Merck, you inherit a legacy with roots in Germany and US operations that date back to 1891. Merck is an example of what Jim Collins wrote about in the best-selling book *Built to Last: Successful Habits of Visionary Companies*. It's Merck's clarity about its social purpose, Larry Fink argues, that enables the company to achieve its full potential.

For companies that raise capital in the public markets, a clear understanding about what matters most helps them withstand short-term demands for higher returns that come at the expense of long-term focus.

A colleague, friend, and adviser, David Langstaff, founded the company Veridian in 1997 and built it into a premier provider of technology solutions and security services to the defense industry. The origins of the company go back much further, to a company with close ties to the space program that David had joined a decade earlier and ultimately managed from a business and operating perspective. I first met David in 1998 as I was transitioning from the Ford Foundation to start the Business and Society Program at the Aspen Institute. We met at a seminar called "The 21st Century Corporation," which explored tensions inherent in the age of globalization, from increasingly complex supply chains to the challenge of attaining higher labor standards and protecting human rights in nation-states with fragile governments and little adherence to the rule of law.

The seminar helped me begin to connect the dots between my work at the Ford Foundation and the values of business leaders able to embrace complexity and to question their place in society. David, it turned out, was attending to learn the discipline of the Aspen seminar as he prepared to join the corps of expert moderators. He was, in my book, already enlightened—but still curious. We stayed in touch, and when it came time to build an advisory board, David agreed to become the chair.

David thinks in terms of inputs and outputs. He believes that the purpose and vision and strategy are the key inputs. As with Roy Vagelos of Merck, for David and the business he was building, a people-centered strategy rooted in values was the key to success and helped him attract the best talent in a competitive industry—and one in which trust was the foundation of business relationships. Seventy-five percent of Veridian's employees had security clearances. The outputs are the goods and services rendered, profits, and other forms of measurable value. Purpose is an input. Profits are an output.

A sign of David's success as a business builder who was deeply comfortable talking about the values of his company came soon after he took Veridian public in 2002. David barely found his legs as the CEO of a public company before the company was in play. The services Veridian provided were a compelling fit for major defense contractors. The offer that finally tipped the balance came from General Dynamics, a $15 billion defense giant. They sought the suite of capabilities—and talent—that Veridian represented in technology-based defense solutions and made an attractive offer for the stock of the company.

Left to his own devices, David would have resisted the tender, but the advisory firms that knocked on his door were quick to insist on the need to prioritize what was best for the shareholders. The purchase price offered by General Dynamics was the highest ever seen by a company like Veridian. It would put a lot of money in the pockets of investors in the company's stock. Cash out today, or continue to build for the future, with the potential of greater returns over time? David sought alternatives. Was financial return the only measure of success, and how could you capture in a spreadsheet the unique capabilities of a company as important to national security as Veridian? What would become of the signature values he wove into decision-making and commitment to his customers—and the team he had built over the course of a decade?

How do you capture the real value in a single number? Or, as the Harvard Business School case written about the decision that David faced at Veridian put it, how do you put a value on values?

The business ultimately was purchased by General Dynamics at a 75 percent premium; 80 percent of the shareholders agreed to the sale, and the company was absorbed into two large divisions of General Dynamics. The law on the fiduciary duty of boards during change of control—aka the Revlon rule—continues to be debated, but today it is no longer assumed that the cash value to shareholders is the only, or the most important, factor in a tender offer. Under Delaware law, the de facto standard for corporate governance law, the board has the freedom to exercise judgment about what is in the long-term interest of the company—to accept the offer or pass, accordingly. And while the story of Veridian and David's emphasis on *values* as the glue in attracting the best talent and commercial success is compelling as the ultimate source of value creation, his vision was never fully tested as a public company. Within a short period of time, David and the core of talented individuals he had built into a highly competitive team had moved on.

In David Langstaff's experience, it's when *profits* get confused with *purpose* that the problems begin. If purpose is only a statement in the corporate social responsibility (CSR) report, it's only a matter of time before the real purpose of the enterprise is revealed.

In September 2016, the chief executive of Wells Fargo, John Stumpf, appeared before a congressional committee and apologized for the high-pressure sales tactics that led to phony fees and accounts and the eventual firing of more than 5,000 employees. It's a matter of debate whether the fired employees were culpable, but what is clear is that the real purpose of the enterprise—profit and stock price—was made apparent through management protocols and incentive systems. Facebook's business model of selling customer data (earning

Purpose and Value Creation

At an event at the Brookings Institution, David Langstaff, founder of Veridian, spoke about what was for him a defining experience in business, one that put him on the path to being a superior executive and leader:

> Early in my career, I joined a company called Space Industries, where I had the good fortune to work with some of the leaders of the nascent US space program—the people to whom President Kennedy turned to put a man on the moon: Bob Gilruth, Max Faget, and Chris Kraft, to name a few. I was struck by how these accomplished people would speak about the Apollo program—how it represented the most satisfying time of their lives. The reason: they were contributing to something that mattered; they were part of a grand adventure that was bigger than any one of them; they had a sense of contribution, responsibility, and purpose that went well beyond their paycheck. Something at the most human level was being addressed.
>
> I expanded on these lessons in building Veridian, and I bring the same approach to TASC [the private company that David ran after the sale of Veridian]. It is clear for me that a meaningful purpose matters deeply. It is the key to unlocking employee commitment, building a positive operating culture, enhancing productivity, and ultimately, delivering exceptional performance. Most important, a clear purpose provides the foundation for institutional values. When your business depends upon attracting and retaining outstanding people, offering an environment where people are able to commit to a higher purpose than simply their job, and aligning institutional with personal values in such a way that neither is compromised—it's what the Apollo program did for those who worked on it in the 1960s. It addresses a basic human need. Frankly, it amazes me that more corporations today don't understand these connections, nor see the benefits.

the catch phrase, "If you aren't paying for the product, you *are* the product") may be more complex to unwind, but it strikes a similar chord.

The employees of the enterprise don't need to be taught the purpose. They live it.

WHAT IS THE PURPOSE OF BOEING?

What is the purpose of Boeing? The company's muddled mission statement might have foretold the company's crisis that *Fortune* called "a scandal of its own making."

At this writing, the Boeing 737 Max, the company's newest jetliner, is still grounded. The order from the FAA came in early 2019 after 346 people died in two separate crashes, each linked to problems with the plane's software. The scrutiny from the press, regulators, and Congress was unforgiving and exposed deep-seated problems in the corporate culture, including pressure to ignore warning signs from employees in a race to market.

Boeing lays out its intentions on its website in a series of statements grouped under "Our Vision." It starts with a statement of purpose and mission in which the word Innovation figures repeatedly, as if to be innovative is an end in itself. Likewise, we have the company's Aspiration: to be the "best in aerospace and enduring global industrial champion."

What does it mean to be "the best"—and by what measure does it constitute a worthy purpose?

When we get to the part about Boeing's strategy for achieving its goals, the prescription for the disaster that has befallen the company is laid out in full. There are three main bullet points, including this one: "Sharpen and Accelerate to Win," which, according to press reports, management took seriously—while skipping basic steps in the design process in a race to market against its chief competitor, Airbus.

In a searing exposé, reporters for the *New York Times* made a strong case that the problems at the company go much deeper than bad design for the 737 Max.[1] Boeing, a market leader in the airplane industry and the crown jewel of US manufacturing, failed on two critical steps: first, setting a clear direction that reflects a real understanding of the public license to operate, and second, building the protocols for driving the purpose through the company's core operations and feedback loops.

The idea of linking purpose to the public interest isn't a new idea—or as lofty as it often sounds. The Engineers' Creed, adopted by the National Society of Professional Engineers in 1954, sets this out as one of four promises made: "To place service before profit, the honor and standing of the profession before personal advantage, and the public welfare above all other considerations."

If the professional creed of engineers is not sufficient, Boeing would have been well served to revisit the bible of manufacturing, Total Quality Management (TQM), or its more modern cousin, Lean Six Sigma, which took American manufacturing by storm after its adoption by GE and Motorola in the 1980s. TQM is defined by Investopedia as "the continual process of detecting and reducing or eliminating errors." It may not be the reference point for managers that it once was, but it stands the test of time with its focus on product quality and customer satisfaction, supported by training, management protocols, and metrics. The underlying tenet of continuous improvement helps assure that performance matches intentions.

PURPOSE IS REVEALED

Business purpose begins with intentions but is revealed through the actions and rewards that shape the culture and the decisions for which the company is known—what the company *becomes*. What was Boeing's true purpose? Simply stated, at a critical point in time, it was to Beat Airbus. While conflating profits and purpose, the company lost its way and squandered the trust of the public—and perhaps, even more important, the trust of pilots, who need to be persuaded again to fly the Boeing aircraft, the 737 Max.

By 2020, the CEO had stepped down, and Boeing's future was uncertain.

It reminds me of a *New Yorker* cartoon framed in the hallway of my office: A rag-tag group of children and an elder are huddled around a flickering campfire. They sit in a scorched-earth terrain; the dim light of the campfire gives way to darkness. The characters are disheveled; the mood is dystopian.

"Yes, the planet was destroyed," their guardian explains, "but for a beautiful moment in time, we created a lot of shareholder value."

Short-termism is one by-product of share price maximization and is evident in the decision rules and regulations that govern corporations and capital markets. To fix the system means rethinking the metrics and incentives that make it more attractive to buy back shares of stock rather than invest in worker training. When a company unlocks its real purpose, it clarifies why it exists and how it will measure success. David Langstaff at Veridian found that clarity of purpose makes it easier to cultivate the kind of investors who will support the decisions and trade-offs required to stay on course.

Yet, the pressure in public markets to place profits ahead of long-term value creation is unrelenting.

The idea that companies must serve a clear purpose—more than making money for the shareholders—may still be challenged by some, but it's hardly a new idea. It's what I like to think former General Motors CEO Charles Wilson meant in 1953 when he told the US Senate that if he was confirmed as secretary of defense, the interests of the nation would come first—but also that he did not truly perceive the potential for conflict: "Because for years I thought what was good for the country was good for General Motors and vice versa."*

The last decades have injected more than a note of irony in this statement, but Wilson was hardly the last executive to feel this way. Many corporations offer evidence that the public interest is still a critical organizing principle for business.

---

*It is worth noting that Charles Wilson is often misquoted as having said, "What's good for General Motors is good for America."

Successful public companies from the Container Store to Herman Miller to JetBlue to Microsoft to Panera Bread and many more are clear about their public purpose. But what sets the successful ones apart isn't the purpose statement itself, it's the follow-through.

Lars Sørensen of Novo Nordisk was named best-performing CEO by *Harvard Business Review* in 2015 and again in 2016. Sørensen describes the juggernaut of the company's success in this way: a premium on values, consensus, and teamwork—and, importantly, a governance structure that offers some protection from the unrelenting pressure of capital markets. In an interview with *HBR*'s editor, Sørensen states:

> Our philosophy is that corporate social responsibility is nothing but maximizing the value of your company over a long period of time, because in the long term, social and environmental issues become financial issues. There is really no hocus-pocus about this. And Novo Nordisk is part-owned by a Danish foundation that obliges us to maximize the value of the company for the long term.[2]

When Sørensen claims that CSR "is nothing but maximizing the value of your company over a long period of time," he elevates time frame as the fulcrum for setting intentions. He also raises the question of ownership and whether public companies have the freedom to succeed over the long haul.

BACK TO THE BASICS

Why do we offer any company the license to operate, the protection of limited liability, and even constitutional rights, such as the freedom to speak in the public square, if the fundamental purpose is more about private inurement than the public good—if the purpose of the firm does not speak clearly to its social utility or fully reward the contributors to the company's success?

Bill Budinger founded Rodel, Inc., with his brother Don. The company that the brothers built together and ultimately sold is still a global leader in high-precision materials and technology for the electronics industry.

Bill has been involved in the Aspen Institute for decades. His interests are wide-ranging, from philosophy and the humanities to energy policy, politics to corporate governance. He is a humble guy; when you share a meal with him, you would never know that he holds more than three dozen patents, including one or more for technology that was instrumental in bringing semiconductor manufacturing back to the United States in the 1990s.

Bill's keen interest in politics grew out of his direct experience in shaping US patent law. The Rodel Fellowship that he envisioned and brought to fruition at the Aspen Institute is an oasis for politicians motivated to work across party lines in a world beset by partisan warfare. I made it my business to get to know Bill based on comments he made at an Aspen Board of Trustees meeting. He is an articulate and impassioned spokesperson on the consequences of shareholder primacy—and for building a business foundation that honors the public license to operate.

For Bill, like Roy Vagelos at Merck and David Langstaff at Veridian, the animating force behind his company's success was about attracting and retaining talent.

Bill has a wry sense of humor. He speaks plainly from his experience as an entrepreneur. A favorite of Bill's many aphorisms is the following: "Profits are a lot like oxygen—clearly necessary. *But to breathe is not what gets anyone out of bed in the morning.*" For Rodel, the investment in talent was key to the culture of innovation that drove the company's success.

Today, it seems that everyone from SEC commissioners to politicians to CEOs rails about short-termism, even as supportive protocols—from the tenor of quarterly conference calls to pay practices—reinforce short-term thinking in practice. Where is the lever for change? And can public companies rise to the challenges of social upheaval and environmental risk—or does that require a protective ownership structure like the one that Novo Nordisk enjoys?

Business executives in public companies operate under remarkable pressure to maximize profits for short-term gain. The *New Yorker* cartoon in my office hallway perfectly captures the choices facing executives now: "Yes, the planet was destroyed, but for a beautiful moment in time, we created a lot of shareholder value." The leverage point for systemic change is where theory and practice meet—the mindsets of leaders on the front lines. What we need is a pronounced shift away from shareholder-centric thinking.

When the Business Roundtable (BRT) renounced shareholder value as the organizing principle of public companies in a statement released in 2019, it was like the shot heard round the world.[3] The announcement came in the sultry days of late August, but my in-box exploded like fireworks on the Fourth of July. *Game over*, I thought. The change in mindset had been unfolding for years, under the mantle of extraordinary leadership in remarkable companies and the insight of scores of thought leaders, activists, and scholars, but now, with the right voices and a large microphone—190 executives of our largest companies—it resounded with éclat.

It was a new day.

The theory-turned-ideology that puts shareholders at the center of the business, which was advanced by scholars in the mid-1980s but quickly took over classrooms, boardrooms, and markets, had begun to shred. A new rule has emerged and will continue to be informed by the practices of great companies.

THE END OF SHAREHOLDER PRIMACY

In 2017, two years before the Business Roundtable's statement emerged, the *Harvard Business Review* published "The Error at the Heart of Corporate Leadership," by two long-time professors at Harvard Business School, Lynn Sharp Paine and Joseph Bower. The article nicely foreshadowed the Business Roundtable's announcement.

Ira Millstein, nonagenarian and esteemed adviser to boards during his long tenure at the New York law firm of Weil, Gotshal

& Manges, called to say the article had him "dancing a jig." Henry Schacht, who had served as CEO of two public companies, Cummins Engine and Lucent Technologies, had the article in his hand when he greeted me several days later in his midtown office. "This is the most important article *HBR* published," he said. "*HBR* blew it by not making it the cover story."

I sent it to everyone I knew.

What makes the Bower-Paine article powerful? It is a well-reasoned critique of shareholder primacy by renowned scholars of business, published in an influential management journal. The authors give executives and boards a fresh way to think about their role—one that appeals to common sense about how businesspeople want to spend their time—building businesses. Put simply, Bower and Paine assert that the *duty of directors is to the health of the enterprise itself*—not to shareholders, who are widely considered to "own the company" and receive both privileges and protections, yet in no way, legally or practically, do they own anything more than shares of stock with specific rights.

Bower and Paine give appropriate credit to law professor Lynn Stout, whose many scholarly articles and books, especially *The Shareholder Value Myth: How Putting Shareholders First Harms Investors, Corporations, and the Public*, helped bring the debate about corporate purpose out of the shadowy domain of corporate governance and onto the main stage.

Professor Stout's great gift was her willingness to challenge the academy on ideology so ingrained that it was no longer truly viewed as theory—without losing the plotline for her real audience: business executives, investor relations professionals, directors of mutual funds, and the rest of us trying to make sense of the constant refrain that "the law makes me do it."

Stout, who tragically died in 2019 of an aggressive cancer, wrote,

> United States corporate law does not, and never has, required directors of public corporations to maximize shareholder wealth. To the

contrary, as long as boards do not use their powers to enrich themselves, the law gives them a wide range of discretion to run public corporations with other goals in mind, including growing the firm, creating quality products, protecting employees, and serving the public interest. Chasing shareholder value is a managerial choice—not a legal requirement.[4]

When the BRT's announcement came out, had she been alive to hear it, she would likely have made a huffy remark, something along the lines of "It's about time," but more biting and memorable, and then returned to her real passion, deconstructing the scaffolding of beliefs and protocols that keep shareholder primacy in place, and coaching scholars and teachers and advocates who had taken up her cause. As a member of our Advisory Board, she always had time for me, but she was never shy about insisting that I could do more, move faster, take on a bolder idea or challenge, right up to the last days of her illness.

The last time I saw Lynn was one week before she died. We were attending the annual meeting of an organization that promotes long-term thinking, called Focusing Capital on the Long Term. She rose to her feet, with the help of a cane, to challenge a respected investor on the stage who hadn't gotten the memo on the purpose of the corporation and had slipped lazily into the mantra about shareholder value as the goal of the enterprise.

Lynn cogently made mincemeat of his words and sat down again.

Her insight about fiduciary duty—that the board's allegiance is to the company itself, rather than to the sea of shareholders with conflicting time horizons and competing goals—firmly links corporate law with common sense.

Shareholders come in many flavors, with diverse interests and investment horizons. The influence of some shareholders over boards is undeniable, but as we will explore in chapter 5, capital is no longer a scarce resource, and the needs of shareholders are not, nor should they be, the primary interest of companies with a long-term view. As Marjorie Kelly wrote in 2001 in her first book, *The Divine Right of*

Capital: Dethroning the Corporate Aristocracy, the company got their money at the IPO. Shareholder primacy is a theory with a stranglehold on finance classrooms, but it is not the law.

US law supports the decision that Roy Vagelos made at the helm of Merck. It ties together David Langstaff's belief that values-based leadership builds real value and Herb Kelleher's management ethic at Southwest Airlines, and that of Unilever's Paul Polman.

The job of public company directors is a lot like the duties of the co-op board where my husband and I own shares. We get to vote in the election of the board, and our shares entitle us to control our premises and to sell to another occupant, but we don't own the building itself—the East End Avenue Corporation does. The co-op's directors like to make their shareholders happy, but their duty is to the long-term preservation of value for the co-op.

The writings of Lynn Stout, Lynn Paine, and Joe Bower describe the legal theory that supports the practices of well-run companies. Their common-sense approach reinforces managers who are keen to focus on what matters most to the long-term health of the enterprise.

The Bower-Paine article also illustrates how business scholars ply their trade—making observations and posing questions rooted in data about the performance of business and markets, which in turn stimulates new lines of inquiry by the next generation of academics, and so on. This is the system of thought leadership at work, from which the business academy derives its influence and the authority to shape the thinking of hundreds of thousands of future businesspeople each year.

From the work of many, a new narrative about the purpose of the corporation and a more useful formulation of the fiduciary duty of boards are taking root.

When the Business Roundtable weighed in on the debate about corporate purpose, it was as if the one wood block that had been keeping the Jenga tower of shareholder-first thinking aloft was *finally dislodged*. The tower of misplaced trust and entrenched ideology came tumbling down with a crash.

The Business Roundtable soundly and firmly retracted the emphasis on the shareholder as the key to value creation, returning to more of a so-called stakeholder view that embraces multiple interests that are critical to business success.

The statement is powerful. It not only retracts shareholder primacy; it raises the bar on business leaders. We are invited to view the CEO signatories as responsible and capable parties with choices to make—choices that have profound impacts on the workplace, on the communities where they work, and well beyond.

Jamie Dimon, CEO of JPMorgan Chase, in his role as chairman of the BRT (who a year earlier said that releasing quarterly earnings forecasts "forces people inside the company to bullshit up the chain"), and Alex Gorsky of Johnson & Johnson, who chaired the BRT Corporate Governance Committee, raised the bar further with these words in the public release:

> Too often hard work is not rewarded, and not enough is being done for workers to adjust to the rapid pace of change in the economy. If companies fail to recognize that the success of our system is dependent on inclusive long-term growth, many will raise legitimate questions about the role of large employers in our society.

The BRT made sure that the statement would be read widely—even in late August, when the denizens of Wall Street take a deep breath and decamp for the beach or the countryside.

The release went viral. From my own perch on an island 10 miles off the coast of New Hampshire, I sat in amazement as messages and headlines flooded my in-box. The first one came in at 6 a.m. from a business school classmate: "Have you seen this????" The headlines focused on the resounding change in what felt like an entrenched idea. Was business really changing its tune about putting shareholders first?

Amid a wave of positive reaction, criticism of the Business Roundtable's bold move was swift and sharp—and came from both the capitalists and the critics of business. Who would hold the companies accountable, if not their shareholders? And how were companies to make decisions among competing demands?

But then also, why should we believe that anything would change?

Distrust in business has been building for decades, from Occupy Wall Street to the techlash to critique on the campaign trail. It is fueled by spectacular examples of business failure, from the implosion of Enron in the early 2000s up to the tale of woe at Boeing almost two decades later. Behaviors like earnings management, underinvestment in infrastructure, tax avoidance, and outsized CEO pay packages, plus the stew of stagnant wages, self-dealing in Washington, and environmental disasters, have produced a resounding chorus of discontent and demand for a new governing ethic.

CREATING REAL VALUE

A few weeks after the release of the Business Roundtable's restatement of corporate purpose, a Bloomberg reporter called for comment on a story he was crafting. When he and I spoke, his colleagues had already interviewed 21 of the 181 executives who initially signed on to the BRT's statement at the time it was first released. The Bloomberg team would continue to probe, but the pattern was already clear. Those interviewed agreed that nothing would really need to change. Signing on was easy to do—they already were doing it. They were attending to the needs of all of their stakeholders.

Pat Gross, a seasoned director and member of our Advisory Board, shared that 75 percent of the directors at a forum he attended had agreed that the new BRT articulation reflected the status quo, that their companies already took a long-term perspective.

What might this mean? What are the steps that can turn a bold move and call to action by the Business Roundtable into a moment of real reflection in boardrooms and executive offices?

How do we leverage this moment?

First, we need to unpack the word *stakeholder*. Roy Vagelos didn't think of the scientists and engineers he hired as stakeholders. Good science was the foundation of long-term success—the organizing principle for the operating model. To make the best decision for the firm, he had to walk in the shoes of the scientists who were critical to the company's growth.

Second, the signatories who say that nothing needs to change confuse important activities and good works with the underlying decision rules and values that determine how to allocate capital and shape attitudes and behaviors. They conflate inputs and outputs. They are failing to look carefully at the *design* of the business model itself—of the business *system*. What key assumptions and nonnegotiables exist in the competitive environment? What is core and what is expendable?

Stakeholders is a grab-bag term that requires deeper thinking to create real value over time. Otherwise, "stakeholder engagement" will continue to be the sole provenance of managers in the social impact office or company foundation. What is needed is to *engage* these strategists with the business heads to help connect purpose, strategy, and capital allocation.

Yes, of course companies invest in the institutions and communities where they work, and yes, they care about their employees and try to connect with the attitudes and preferences of millennials and the like. But to reverse decades of mistrust, to ensure that we are on a different path, requires a level of authenticity that must be the rule, not the exception.

The list of leaders managing with a new mandate is growing.

On his first day on the job in 2009, Paul Polman, CEO of Unilever, dropped the practice of "guiding" the market of stock pickers and called on his CEO peer group to follow suit. Unilever's long-term orientation and plan to grow the business for the benefit of all who contribute drew committed investors and scores of job applicants, and created sufficient goodwill to withstand an unfriendly bid for the company in 2017. He was supremely popular with the CSR set for his Sustainable Living Plan, but he also enriched the shareholders that were along for the ride.

Polman joined a growing cadre of CEOs who have new answers to timeless questions: How does the company measure success—and over what time frame? What constitutes a high-quality decision that stands the test of time? Who is "downstream" from the business and needs to be consulted in order to assess—and mitigate—risk and eliminate negative externalities?

From Herb Kelleher's phenomenal legacy at Southwest Airlines to Marc Benioff's provocative leadership style and provocative questions about equity at Salesforce, Satya Nadella's turnaround of the fortunes of Microsoft and commitment to carbon recapture, Tom Wilson of Allstate's declaration on workers and jobs, and Indra Nooyi's innovative pursuit of a healthier product mix at Pepsi—these and many fresh faces in the C-suite are opening the door to new questions and expectations about business and its role in society.

The tension between profits today and real value creation over time persists, but *the narrative about the purpose of the corporation—* taught in MBA classrooms and accepted as the first principle in boardrooms—has clearly changed. The strong reactions to the BRT statement demonstrate just how big a shift in attitudes and mindset is already underway.

Jeff Weiner, the inquisitive and thoughtful leader of LinkedIn, spoke to a group of Aspen Institute Fellows in fall 2019, shortly before announcing that he would leave the company in 2020. Jeff was CEO for over a decade of rapid growth and through its acquisition by Microsoft in 2016. He talked about the pursuit of talent, technology, and trust. "What are we trying to accomplish, and how are we going to accomplish it?" Simple questions, but complex in execution. Authenticity, he said, is about keeping your promises; it is about actions, not words.

The BRT's decision to walk back into the public square and remind us of corporate America's intention to honor its license to operate was important because of the dialogue it enabled. But to restore trust requires us to revisit the fundamentals.

What Matters Most? BRT and Purpose:
The Key Tests of Business Commitment

What is the true measure of business success? How do we know if a company places the public interest squarely at the center of decision-making? What would be the signs of authentic commitment to the principles of management released by the BRT? We will not find the answers in the generic surveys that crowd the in-boxes of CSR professionals. What matters most, *in fact*? The most relevant questions are challenging but revealing:

- How much does the company spend on **tax avoidance**? Does it engage in transfer pricing schemes that assign value to low-tax or no-tax havens to avoid higher taxes where the product is designed and produced?

- What purpose is served by **share buybacks**, and under what conditions are they initiated?

- How do the company's **lobbyists** spend their time? What is the platform of trade groups working in the name of the company; does it jibe with stated values and policy—from climate change to inequality?

- What story would be, could be, told about **job creation and worker investment**? What is the company trying to accomplish when it outsources jobs, and are there lines of sight into the wages, benefits, and opportunities for those who work in the company's name but are not on the payroll?

- What is the return to shareholders versus the return to real value creators? Does everyone participate in a **profit-sharing** plan, or is it reserved for key executives and managers? Who benefits the most from the profits and cash generated by the business?

And of course, **what is the CEO paid to do**? Is some version of total shareholder return the loudest signal in the pay package?

To create and sustain real value begins with clarity of purpose but then requires a closer look at the decision rules and protocols—the scaffolding that keeps shareholder-centric thinking in place. Both scholars and executives are called to illuminate and then activate a more robust, socially useful conception of the firm.

The change is underway and is irreversible. The pressure to think differently, to embrace a new set of rules, emerges from changes in a society hungry for leadership from the private sector and from changes within the ranks of employees on a mission to connect their jobs to what they hold dear.

As the next chapter illustrates, the new rules are often dictated by agents who operate from far outside the gates of the business itself, whose work to reverse the decline of endangered species or tackle the roots of climate change focuses their attention on global corporations—their buying power and contract relationships, complexity, and capacity.

They seek out business executives who are sending out new signals, who can articulate what is expected of them now and what needs to be true to honor the promises made.

◆ OLD RULE ◆
Corporate responsibility is defined by host communities and fence-line neighbors.

A corporation has a social responsibility to create jobs, support local services and civic institutions, and contain pollution.

◆ NEW RULE ◆
Corporate responsibility is defined far outside the business gates.

Corporate responsibility is a moving target. It extends through the supply chain and ecosystem, and even to private use of the products—and is defined by forces outside the corporation's reach and control.

CHAPTER THREE

Responsibility Redefined

RULE #3

Corporate Responsibility Is Defined Far outside the Business Gates

We know a lot about how to manage companies from the inside, but the factors that are going to make firms flourish are increasingly external.

—ROSABETH MOSS KANTER

MY FIRST JOB after college was in the California State Legislature, where I worked as a legislative aide and lobbyist for public interest groups. In 1976, I jumped at the chance to work for Arlen Gregorio, a creative and principled Democratic state senator from San Mateo County who chaired the Senate Health and Welfare Committee. An issue that was beginning to draw the attention of Senate staff was the sale of infant formula by Nestlé to mothers in what we then called the third world, today's emerging markets.

A report published in 1974 by a British NGO called War on Want accused Nestlé of aggressive and deceptive marketing to poor women.

The report was titled *The Baby Killer*, and it accused Nestlé of putting its profits before the health and safety of children in developing countries.

By 1977, protests against the company had morphed into an international boycott fueled by outrage that Nestlé would intercede in what nature offered—breastfeeding the young—to profit from families who could ill afford the cost of artificial milk in a can or box. Infant formula, a popular alternative in the United States to breastfeeding baby boomer children like me, was being marketed in the developing world as a path to better nutrition and baby health, but the concern grew that these women might need to dilute the product too much to make it more affordable or might depend on water that was either scarce or polluted, undermining any possible nutritional benefit. Either way, babies could lose out on the natural immunities conveyed through breastfeeding—or worse. Stories circulated about sales reps wearing nurses' uniforms to gain the confidence of women just trying to do the right thing for their children.

Ad by ad, letter by letter, protest by protest, working through the Catholic sisterhood and networks like the Investor Responsibility Research Center, consumers began to shun Nestlé products while socially motivated investors unloaded Nestlé stock.

It took more than a decade, but with no signs of the boycott losing steam, Nestlé finally bowed to pressure from both campaigners and the World Health Organization. The company pledged to fundamentally rethink its approach to marketing the product outside of the "developed" world, in spite of a great growth opportunity and a lurking question about who decides what products can be offered, where.

Today, Nestlé is a massive enterprise with more than 300,000 employees and 100 brands, operating in nearly 200 countries around the world. A quick Google search will surface both praise and criticism, but the company still bears the scars of a persistent campaign that began over 50 years ago. Marketing practices in specific regions are still monitored against a code of conduct. Type in the words

"Nestlé infant formula," and a half dozen links to stories about the crisis appear.

The Nestlé boycott is an early and remarkable example of campaigners wielding consumer purchasing power and investment to influence global brands. The boycott demonstrates the power of networks positioned far outside the gates of the business or the halls of the legislature. Progress was slow, but the highly committed campaigners eventually succeeded in their quest.

What happens when the same networks are powered by the speed of the Internet?

In the mid-1990s, Greenpeace launched a strike to expose Shell's plans to sink an abandoned oil platform in the North Sea. Even before broad access to cell phones and the Internet, the news spread so quickly and powerfully that it was reported that Shell sales at the gas pump in Germany had declined by half.

In another rich example from the same era, Nike's reputation plummeted as a toxic combination of facts and rumors about the company's dependence on unsavory labor practices took hold in the media. As the Internet expanded from its base within research universities to Silicon Valley and then, with the advent of search engines, into businesses, homes, and schools, the campaigners gained a powerful tool.

For Nike, the mere hint of children working in sweatshops to produce shoes became a serious concern for the key market for their product, teenagers. The impact on sales was never clear, but reports of softening in consumer demand finally hit their mark, and in 1998, Nike's cofounder and CEO, Phil Knight, was compelled to speak out on allegations of bad conduct deep in the supply chain.

Once he had gone public about the issues that the company was facing, there was no pulling back. Knight announced a set of measures to enhance Nike's code of conduct and extensive protocols for managing relationships with remote contractors. In doing so, the company raised the bar within its industry. The brand is still a lightning rod for public opinion, but the actions taken, and the commitment to

execution over the long haul, largely restored the company's reputation. Before Nike announced these measures, only Levi Strauss had
a policy that extended standards at home to its foreign contractors.

Years later, Shell was once again the principal target of a publicity
campaign. This one rode the wave of social media and aimed at the
environmental costs of drilling in the Alaskan Arctic. A three-year
campaign of eye-catching, media-friendly acts of individual sabo-
tage—from climbing the Shard in London to hanging from rigs and
bridges in the Pacific Northwest to hacking the Shell-sponsored Formula One awards ceremony—caused Shell in 2015 to vacate its plans
to drill in Alaska.

Greenpeace is an environmental organization with offices in more
than 50 countries around the world. It excels at employing media.
In the campaign against Shell, it once ran a clever video featuring a
polar bear made of Lego blocks, stranded in a polluted Artic, to bring
the costs of drilling into the living rooms of millions who would never
wave a flag or scale a building. By one count, as many as six million
individuals responded. Shell received at least a million emails implor-
ing the company to stop the drilling.

Every step ignites and illuminates the power of the World Wide Web.

For companies caught in the crosshairs of a public protest, social
media is a complex game. The *target* of the boycott may have only an
indirect connection to the underlying motivation for protest. In 2017,
Uber was singled out after a newly elected President Trump signed an
order to stop citizens of seven Muslim-majority nations from entering
the United States.

When taxi drivers, including many who hailed from Pakistan and
Bangladesh, joined in solidarity with protesters converging on air-
ports across the country, the demand for Uber airport pickups quickly
grew. Uber's pricing, which automatically increases in response to a
surge in demand, angered customers who just needed a way to get to
or from the airport—and protesters shunned the drivers for tacitly
supporting the president's move against immigration. The fact that

Uber's CEO, Travis Kalanick, was a member of the president's newly organized business council didn't help matters.

A campaign to delete the Uber ride-hailing app swiftly emerged on social media, and #DeleteUber became a vehicle for public outrage at the White House's stance on immigration. Hundreds of thousands deleted the app, at least for a few days, and for reasons that spanned a host of concerns about the company, its culture, and its controversial CEO.

What was Uber to do? The decision of the president of the United States to ban citizens of foreign nations from entering the country sits way outside the control of the CEO of Uber or any other company. Yet his own employees began to speak up, and within days, Kalanick announced that he was stepping down from the president's council. When other CEOs followed suit, the newly created business advisory group was disbanded.

But is Uber, or Shell, a bad actor?

By some measures, Shell has the best reputation in its industry. Royal Dutch Shell is headquartered in Holland and incorporated in Britain. Shell mirrors the values and sensibility of its European home base. This became clear when the company spoke out on the need for action on climate change in the early 2000s, a decade or more before its US competitors began to take the issue to heart.

Fast-forward to 2018, when Royal Dutch Shell CEO Ben van Beurden called climate change "the most important discussion of our time" and announced aggressive goals for reducing carbon emissions, investment in renewables, and advancing technology to rapidly charge electric vehicles. Shell leaped ahead of competitors again in 2019 when it quit the American Fuel and Petrochemical Manufacturers trade association over differences on climate policy, and once again by detailing aspirations for net-zero carbon emissions throughout the company's operations and expressing the intention to require offsets on the use of Shell products by wholesale customers in the manufacturing, airline, and shipping sectors.

Yet, in the age of the Internet, a brand as visible as Shell is also a convenient and tactical bull's-eye. Greenpeace and Oxfam, another highly networked global NGO, can't rally consumer power against a company we have never heard of.

Sophisticated campaigns of activist or grassroots organizations succeed because they are able to link an urgent need for massive change in the harvesting or production of faceless commodities, or in the working conditions of laborers and service workers, to the consumer brands that depend on them. In one remarkably complex example, Oxfam launched a campaign to tie the burning of forests in Indonesia to make way for expansion of palm oil plantations—to cookies made with Nestlé cocoa and lotions and cosmetics sold by Unilever. The winning formula relies on social media to stir up consumer outrage against brands with high-asset value. The underlying goal is to motivate consumer product companies to demand change from miners, developers, refiners, transporters, and manufacturers with no brand to protect. In between the consumer-facing companies and the commodity producers lie local and national governments, international agencies that oversee trade and product standards, consortia with their own codes of conduct, and workers just trying to put food on the table.

Phil Knight of Nike, in a speech before the National Press Club in 1998, put it simply: "The Nike product has become synonymous with slave wages, forced overtime, and arbitrary abuse. I truly believe that the American consumer does not want to buy products made in abusive conditions."[1]

Don Tapscott, a visionary thinker who seems to see around corners, started writing and speaking about the impact of new media years before the age of a communications tool in every pocket. In the book he coauthored with David Ticoll, *The Naked Corporation: How the Age of Transparency Will Revolutionize Business*, Tapscott archly captures the business risks of what he calls radical transparency: "If you are going to be naked," he warns, "you had better be buff."[2]

Nestlé. Nike. Shell. Unilever. Each of these examples demonstrates how the rules of engagement that link global brands and local labor and environmental standards are changing in real time—and are determined by forces outside the control of the executive. What might have seemed like normal business practices one day can morph into a new norm, seemingly overnight. The early stages of a sophisticated campaign may be invisible to the C-suite. When it emerges on social media, it takes the company by storm.

My daughter Anna came home from high school one day reporting that kids in her homeroom had sworn off M&Ms because they were tied to child labor. This was 2001; reports of West African children bonded to small cocoa farmers in the Ivory Coast were hitting the mainstream press, but facts were elusive. I tried to explain that the issue was a lot more complicated than a single company that might, or might not, be linked to unsavory labor practices. In fact, if her friends were trying to join the boycott-du-jour, they needed to do more research to make sure they had the right company.

It reminds me of the game of Telephone we played at birthday parties when I was a kid. A mix of facts and rumors spreads like wildfire, and global companies invest in rapid-response communications systems to both tell their story and keep an eye on events that could disrupt business operations overnight. The best ones scrub their supply chains to identify and eliminate weak links—such as contractors whose performance would not hold up well under public scrutiny. The companies have a valuable asset to protect—corporate reputation affects access to talent, investment capital, and the actual license to operate locally and globally.

But rumors aside, there are plenty of examples of business excess, greed, and short-term behavior to digest. Traditional news sources, blogs, and late-night television programs shower us with examples. They put my trust in business and markets to the test.

REDEFINING RESPONSIBILITY:
THE BUSINESS RESPONSE

In a global economy, the role of the traditional standard-setters is in flux—especially against the backdrop of growth in social media and Internet-enabled networks and NGOs operating at a great remove from the company. Governments may set the most basic rules, but these new forces that exist outside of commerce and government are better equipped to raise the bar on business practices—to ratchet up the norms and protocols and see that they migrate into the competitive environment.

Corporate responsibilities have grown to include not just the supply chain but the entire ecosystem of inputs and actors. Before Phil Knight gave his speech, the standards of contractors in foreign countries were someone else's problem. The lines between strict legal liability and morality continue to blur as the understanding of corporate responsibility extends even to the personal habits and private use of products in the consumer's own home. Gun manufacturers and bartenders have already felt the pressure. The list of products linked to social consequences—from soda to cell phones—is growing.

NGOs and loose confederations of networks have little to lose. The rules that define the company's footprint are set far from headquarters. How will companies deal with this reality?

The courage of a teen-aged Swedish climate campaigner, Greta Thunberg; the fiery commitment of Emma González and her classmates in Parkland, Florida, who turned grief into political action in the wake of the mass shooting at their high school—these individuals put a fresh face on the word *future*. They enlist millions of voices and, by extension, raise public consciousness and expectations about business's role.

But when it comes to translating that energy, to converting public expectations into product design or the protocols of sustainable development, the greatest levers are deployed at the *precompetitive* level. Agents of change know to enlist business competitors who in turn can influence the standards of shared producers, even before the first purchase order is issued.

In a compelling TED Talk, environmentalist Jason Clay offers up the math behind the strategy pursued by his employer, WWF, and peer organizations with the staying power to lead systemic change.[3] He drills down from the broad scope of the consuming public to precise levers in the supply chain. There are 6.9 billion consumers on the planet and 1.5 billion business-to-consumer producers that supply their needs. Yet it's a much smaller number of global marketers and traders of key commodities who set the rules that ensure—or destroy—biodiversity.

Jason at WWF focuses on 15 basic products—including farmed salmon, cotton, and palm oil—commodities with an outsized impact on places where biodiversity is threatened, from rainforests to the spawning grounds of specific fish vulnerable to extinction. Jason and his co-conspirators then map out companies, numbering in the hundreds, that represent the lion's share of the buying and selling of those commodities.

At the end of this funnel, as few as 100 companies touch multiple commodities and are deemed the most influential in the market. Try to influence the buying habits of seven billion consumers or use those 100 agents to set new rules and standards? As Jason states, it's not easy to build effective working groups across fiercely competitive producers and industries, but it's an easy choice to make.

At the heart of the change is the reality of business risk.

Companies face risk of interruptions to their supply chain, fueled by climate change, media, or economic and political unrest. They face costly risks to their reputations in consumer markets, but also in credit, investor, and labor markets. These disruptions pummel big industrial firms with massive footprints, but also the consumer brands and retailers, from Tiffany to Procter & Gamble to Walmart.

The disruptions extract tremendous cost when consumers reject the product or governments reject the business model—from California's mandate that Uber put independent drivers on the payroll with benefits, to Amazon's failed bid to win New York City's support—and subsidy—for a massive expansion in Queens, to numerous challenges to Facebook's highly profitable but morally questionable use of artificial intelligence to customize and target commercial and political advertising.

THE STORY OF CHANGE

The strategy and tactics deployed to influence a B2B corporation like Maersk, the global shipping line, or Dow, the chemical manufacturer, are different than for consumer businesses. Either way, the early adopter or first mover—the company that raises the bar and sets a new course for its industry—is responding to a complicated stew of both instrumental and intrinsic motivations.

In 2001, we hosted a group of business executives and scholars on the Aspen Institute campus to consider the role of business in leading change—specifically the question of how more enlightened standards of behavior evolve and become common practice. Roger Martin expanded on the ideas that the group explored in a 2002 *Harvard Business Review* article titled "The Virtue Matrix."[4]

Examples like Merck and the campaign to end river blindness demonstrate *intrinsic* motivation—when the financial value to the company's shareholders or investors of a socially beneficial practice or investment is either negative or intangible—i.e., hard to capture in dollars and cents. But Martin and colleagues went further to map how a conscious choice in one company can start to build a higher foundation for a sector or industry—and reward a first mover as well as strengthen the foundation for positive change.

Another example of the return on doing the right thing was playing out in real time. When the Aspen dialogue took place, the HIV-AIDS epidemic was still a major threat. Patients in the United States were able to access promising treatments, but the cost of therapy was a massive burden to families and partners. Prudential Insurance Company decided to allow victims of HIV to access the cash value of their life insurance policies, so-called viatical benefits, to support their care. The decision was well received, and competitors soon followed suit, but that was far from a given when Prudential took what looked like an uncompetitive financial risk.

Costco's elevated wage rates, Patagonia's commitment to organic cotton farming, Southwest's passion for employees, Chipotle's introduction of healthy and sustainable products to the fast-casual food industry—each required initial investment and higher operating costs, motivated by market positioning and at least the potential for competitive advantage. The payback comes through heightened reputation among consumers, investors, and employees. For B2B companies—mining, extractives, utilities—the license to operate granted by countries or local jurisdictions and the dependent relationships with retailers and producers are what elevate behavior. These enterprises are rooted to place; it takes decades to realize a return on investment. The license to operate is not just a metaphor—it is linked to a complex set of relationships, behaviors, and expectations that need to stand the test of time.

Successfully raising the bar in an industry while protecting the franchise requires a kind of corporate fitness. It requires continuous and careful management of the core operations of the enterprise—think lean management or TQM, not CSR. It requires delivering on the promise of superior service and being a good neighbor, as well as investments that test the balance between profitability today and long-term competitive advantage.

COMPANIES OPERATE UNDER A MICROSCOPE

The ability to deliver on promises is paramount. Chipotle became the first mass marketer of what they called "Food with Integrity." The company advertised "responsibly raised" meat, poultry, and organic ingredients. With a brand built around these claims, the business becomes vulnerable to challenges from all corners.

A tough year came to a head in fall 2015 when a regional *E. coli* outbreak at Chipotle stores in the Pacific Northwest brought sales to a standstill. The company added new safety procedures, multiple layers of audits, training, discounts, and freebies to restore consumer trust and rebuild the brand—and then created a marketing campaign to remind people and investors why they fell in love with the company to begin with.

PepsiCo has over a billion dollars in brands and operations spanning virtually every country on Earth. Indra Nooyi joined the company in 1994 and was CEO from 2006 until 2018. Her impact on the company's strategy was profound. She leaned in hard to early signs of consumer interest in lower-fat and less sugary products and launched and invested in offerings that balanced the "good for you" with the "fun for you." Marketing dollars were aligned with the new direction. Changing the traditional product mix entailed massive risk in a highly competitive environment. In my occasional visits with her, she spoke in terms of a road race: you need to make a pit stop now and then to refresh and refuel and invest in new capacities, but it's a long race and requires staying power.

The markets didn't like Pepsi messing around with the consumer addiction to soda and scolded Indra for her audacity to put purpose before profits. Nelson Peltz, the corporate raider, paid her a call and threatened a shareholder action to take control and split up the company to extract value. Indra weathered the storm with difficulty, compromising along the way, but she is remembered, even revered, as a feisty, hard-charging leader who knew what she wanted to accomplish and relentlessly pursued her goals. She also changed the conversation about women at the helm.

Indra consistently reminds audiences to focus on how you make your money, not how you give it away. There is a role for philanthropy and good works, but to secure reputation among consumers and build trust with investors and regulators entails careful management of everyone who touches the product, from development to delivery. And that level of vigilance requires a fundamental transformation of business mindset and processes.

Palm Oil—a Story of Change

Driving change in the harvesting of palm oil is one of the linchpins of reducing large-scale deforestation and greenhouse gases produced by growers in Indonesia—the fourth-largest emitter of CO_2, after China, the United States, and Russia. In Indonesia it is common practice to set fires to forests and peatlands to increase the amount of lands for production of this popular vegetable oil.

Rain forests are threatened and cut down for a myriad of reasons, from cattle ranching for beef production in South America to harvesting of mahogany and teak for furniture in Asia. In Indonesia, where roughly 10 percent of the remaining rain forest in the world remains, it's about palm oil.

Palm oil is the most widely produced vegetable oil in the world. It is found in half of the products on grocery shelves; it keeps lipstick and chocolate from melting and is an essential oil in most shampoos. It makes bread easier to bake and adds the creamy texture to ice cream. It is cheap, has thousands of consumer and industrial uses, and is a traded commodity. Forty-five percent of the world's supply is sourced in Indonesia, where deforestation has occurred at an alarming rate. If this is left unchecked, some estimate that there will be no more rain forest in the country by 2030. The impacts on biodiversity, air and water quality, and land erosion and flooding are connected to growth in demand for palm oil.

The supply chain for palm oil is complex. At one end are several million smallholder farmers in Indonesia and beyond, for whom harvesting palm oil is both the livelihood and a cornerstone of the economic success of their communities and region. In addition, major commodity traders like Cargill rely on industrial-scale monocrop plantations that have contributed to burning of forests and displacement of indigenous farmers to keep pace with demand. At the other end are the rest of us, billions of consumers, buying snacks, personal care products, and cleaning agents with mysterious ingredients like *Elaeis guineensis*, sodium laureth sulfate, or palmitoyl oligopeptide.

Engaging the consumer as an agent of change in saving the rain forest is complicated, but the strategy is by now a familiar one and takes us back to the consumer-facing corporation as the key to unlocking protocols and practices that align pocketbooks and beliefs.

Adopting new rules and definitions of responsibility also means listening to internal agents of change. They include the managers who take the calls from small investors and citizen groups that connect products or services to economic realities hidden from those of us who just want to buy a can of tuna or school clothes. These managers can offer early warnings about problems deep in the supply chain that will come home to roost in a generation or less time: degradation of soil; clear-cutting of forests; the loss of biodiversity; water scarcity; even enslaved labor on fishing boats that rarely reach shore, and the securing of bonded labor in hotel rooms in far-flung capitals.

As we will explore in the next chapter, the smart companies understand that their own employees can help. The social networks they join exist at the intersection of product and service delivery and demand for change. They can identify risk and protect the reputation before it is on the line. The new rules may be set elsewhere, but employees are able to lean into a complex dance of local needs, global networks, and personal values and awareness. They think like citizens first—citizens who are too impatient to wait for government to act.

Case examples help us understand just how much the rules of engagement have already changed. They illuminate the motivations, the market pressures, and the role of mediating institutions that connect producer to consumer. The brands are the public face of the tensions and trade-offs between consumers drawn to price and convenience on the one hand, and labor markets and systems collapse on the other.

It's easier to begin a conversation than to get to a critical mass. The actions of a few players determine the outcome for one contest— but the collective action of major players can change the rules of the game. In chapter 6, we see what is required of business when the system itself is at risk of collapse.

WHO LEADS?

The process begins when NGOs apply pressure on the front lines. They unite "teamsters and turtles" to tackle systemic problems: human rights, workplace safety, and fair wages; biodiversity and climate change. The power of social media is catalytic. Changes in protocols and processes in a market leader can redefine choices across entire industries and markets. It requires a steady hand and trusted brokers with a long-term focus. For the front-runners, it also requires respect for the rule of law and agreement among parties that usually compete.

The corporation with global reach and exposure is what is needed to make the changes scale, and stick.

◆ **NEW RULE** ◆

Employees give voice to risk and competitive advantage.

Employees are critical business allies in a changing world; they
identify future risks and see the opportunity embedded in
new norms around sustainability and social responsibility.

CHAPTER FOUR

The Voice of the Employee

RULE #4

Employees Give Voice to Risk and Competitive Advantage

A human management will demand that we incorporate a concern for the freedom and well-being of those we manage as much as for their productivity; that we consider the environmental as well as the economic consequences of strategic choices. . . . That we hear and amplify a broader set of voices, not only those that fit a narrow view of management and of its concerns, but also those that defy it, and in so doing, enliven it.

—GIANPIERO PETRIGLIERI, "ARE OUR MANAGEMENT THEORIES OUTDATED?," *HARVARD BUSINESS REVIEW*

DAN BROSS moved from Washington, DC, to Seattle to join the governmental affairs department of Microsoft in 1998. We were first introduced in 2005, shortly after Dan had been tapped to build out the company's global corporate social responsibility program, a job that included responding to a growing array of increasingly noisy stakeholders with a range of interests and demands.

At that time, Dan was wrestling with the threat of a boycott over the company's position on a controversial bill introduced in the Washington legislature. Microsoft and the Aspen Institute shared a board member in common, Ann McLaughlin Korologos, who had served as labor secretary under President Reagan. She thought a conversation between the two of us might be helpful.

At issue was whether to add sexual orientation to the protected classes listed in the state's equal opportunity statute. The proposed amendment was offensive to a charismatic religious leader in Microsoft's hometown. Dan was seeking a way to anchor Microsoft's support for the bill in broad policy.

I suggested that Dan look into a relatively new business network, the UN Global Compact, an affiliation of companies aligned with the United Nations and its member states on human rights, labor, and environmental protocols. The UN Global Compact framework proved helpful to Dan. As a member of the Compact, Microsoft could support an expansion of the state's equal opportunity law in furtherance of the principles of human rights established at the founding of the UN.

Yet, what really enabled Microsoft to move from passive to active support for the bill was hearing from the company's own employees. The turning point came when an affinity group known by the acronym GLEAM—Gay and Lesbian Employees at Microsoft—began to express strong support for the bill. The group was an acknowledged network within the company, one of its many employee resource centers that link up employees who share common concerns. The network represented highly valued employees; their opinions mattered to Dan and the leadership.

The new era of employee voice and influence had only begun.

In February 2017, a newly elected President Trump declared the United States off-limits to the citizens of seven countries with Muslim majorities. When 160 chief executives of biotech companies published a letter condemning the president's decision, their apprehension crossed the line from professional to personal. Each of these executives had a story to tell; many were immigrants themselves.

But it was the effect of the travel ban on thousands of engineers and other professionals and valued employees who were now at risk that turned antipathy toward Trump's stance into a call to action.

This was not the first time that CEOs were moved to speak out publicly on social policy. In 2015, in the run-up to the 2016 election, Salesforce CEO Marc Benioff created a media storm in a showdown with then-Governor Mike Pence of Indiana over a law that permitted business owners to refuse service to the LGBT community.

"We can't bring our customers or our employees into a situation where they might be discriminated against," Benioff said. "We have a large number of employees and customers who would be impacted dramatically by this legislation . . . I'm really just advocating on their behalf."[1]

In the weeks and months that followed the Muslim ban, more CEOs began to speak out about concerns that their predecessors had eschewed as too risky or outside the bounds of commerce. Merck CEO Ken Frazier resigned from Trump's manufacturing council over the president's tacit approval of white supremacists marching in Charlotte, South Carolina, while a growing epidemic of gun violence caused a chorus of CEOs in retail, consumer brands, and local communities to advocate for gun control. Ed Bastian, CEO of Delta, canceled a group discount proffered to members of the National Rifle Association, and the Georgia legislature retaliated by initially withdrawing a beneficial tax credit. In response to employee concerns, Mark Hoplamazian, CEO of Hyatt, disallowed hate groups listed on a federal watch list from renting meeting space in Hyatt hotels.

Hearing from CEOs on issues even more highly charged than immigration became a common occurrence as chief executives gave voice to workplace and societal norms around tolerance, identity, and equity. And employees, for the most part, responded with enthusiasm. They had been given a voice on issues that they cared about through the words of their own leaders.

It is a short walk from activism in the C-suite to employees speaking for themselves. Unions have been in decline for decades, but the voice of the employees is getting stronger—and they are speaking out not just on issues related to their own well-being but on social issues that affect the company's well-being. There is no dialing back.

ACCOUNTABILITY FROM THE CAFETERIA

The media are steeped in examples of investors and consumers holding companies to account. It's possible to forget that it's the workers who know the company and products best.

Enter a new and powerful accountability mechanism.

Employees are the front lines of customer interface and user experience, and they have a direct understanding of risks in the supply chain. When the firm's culture enables it, employees work to improve efficiency and quality, and speak up on innovation and investment to support future growth. They are the first to know when protocols are ignored and when the enterprise—and its customers or workers—are at risk.

They also have sight lines into the working conditions and financial security of hourly workers, including the contractor in the next cubicle or aisle.

Employees expect their leaders to step up on issues that command our attention in the public square, from inequality to climate change. These grand challenges can be by-products of the business model, and both threaten our economic system and eventually rebound to the health of the business itself. The issues that command the attention of employees today connect business decisions to broad social trends and environmental demands.

Open communication with the workforce is important for all of these reasons, but concern for employees is about more than competitive advantage.

Employees *are* the business—they are not just so-called stakeholders who feel the effects of business decisions or have a legitimate point of view from downstream or outside the gates. The sacrifices made by workers in the COVID-19 pandemic bring this reality home. In an era of instability and economic upheaval, the health and safety of the workforce and financial security of individual contributors, and the complicated balancing act between public welfare and private incentives, are front and center.

The question of who sets the rules of business is an important one. Practically speaking, business interests and their trade groups have won the war against unions, as well as many battles for lower taxes and less government regulation. Yet the accountability mechanisms to make sure that the norms and decision rules work for business and work for society are being reexamined. As my Aspen Institute colleague Maureen Conway, head of the Institute's Economic Opportunities Program, asks, "Is this business victory really best for business in the long term?"

The employees' role in holding business to account derives from critical engagement in the *purpose* of the enterprise—the delivery of goods and services. Under the new rules of engagement, employees are no longer viewed as a cost of doing business. In fact, the value of committed employees defies measurement. Unquestionably, today, and hopefully for a long time into the future, the conversation is now about the workers' *humanity*.

Gianpiero Petriglieri teaches management at INSEAD in Fontainebleau, France. He is also a medical doctor and psychiatrist by training and a provocative contributor to leadership thinking and practice. In a 2020 article in *Harvard Business Review* titled, "Are Our Management Theories Outdated?" he describes a "mid-life crisis" in management—caused by existential questions about capitalism itself. Petriglieri writes, "The worldview that most management theories and tools have long been drafted to sustain and advance—is at an existential juncture. We are no longer just asking how to make it work. Many now wonder why (and for whom) it exists. Some are even asking if it is viable any more."[2]

Petriglieri sees changes already underway and is hopeful that they will result in a form of management that is more human, that encourages both curiosity and compassion, and therefore is much better at both innovation and inclusion:

One can see glimpses of such a human view of management already. You can see them in the CEOs who talk about caring about purpose as much as about profit. You can see them in people's longing for meaning and community at work. But for those claims not to ring hollow and those longings not to go unmet, management as we know it, really, it has to die. There is no other way. Because, in truth, it does not have a problem. It is the problem.

He continues,

We do not need new theories of management. We need a broader purpose for it. And we need that purpose to emerge not in bold pronouncements but in ongoing conversations, with ourselves and others, that challenge instrumental theories. Those conversations are far more useful at existential junctures like this. They are a far better means to free us up and join us in bringing about a human turn in management—and ultimately in our relationships with each other, with technology, and with the planet in the workplace.[3]

The change Petriglieri calls for is already fully engaged.

The trends we are seeing in worker activism and worker voice may seem like a sudden reversal, or maybe a counterpoint, to the steady decline of unions, yet a closer look at the culture of the workplace reveals a different picture. As boomers have exited the workplace over the last decade and made room for younger generations, companies have invested in research to understand the attitudes, motivations, and expectations of those who will move into management roles.

Clay Christensen, the management guru renowned for his observations about "disruptive innovation" and author of the best-selling book *The Innovator's Dilemma: When New Technologies Cause Great Firms to Fail*, opened a new chapter in his life after receiving a cancer diagnosis. In his final book, *How Will You Measure Your Life?* Christensen writes about life choices that no longer divide up easily between office and home. "It's easier to hold your principles 100 percent of the time than it is to hold them 98 percent of the time," he says, talking about values and priorities that contribute to a life of meaning—and cannot, should not, be put aside *just this once*.[4] He could also be speaking about the power of the workplace as a platform for our commitments to the commons.

The extended social isolation period of the COVID-19 pandemic further erased the boundaries between work and home. The term *work-life balance* may no longer be useful.

THE #METOO MOMENT

The networking tools of an efficient and connected workforce and social media conspired to open a new era of employee activism at precisely 11 a.m. on November 1, 2018. More than 20,000 Google employees and contractors worldwide walked off the job. The trigger was how the company handled claims of sexual harassment against a respected and powerful executive.

The company investigated the claims and reportedly found them "credible." The executive in question, Andy Rubin, the so-called Father of the Android, was asked to leave and did, returning to the venture capital firm he had created before his tenure at Google. Years later, when the company confirmed that Rubin had negotiated an exit package of $90 million, the Internet exploded.

Even a careful watch over employee engagement scores failed to anticipate the abrupt changes that would come about through the #MeToo movement and the end of decades of silence by women about harassment in the workplace. The change in power dynamics was felt across institutions, from college campuses to movie studios, in politics and media, and from Wall Street to Silicon Valley.

#GoogleWalkout captured the media by storm, and the company acquiesced to some of the employees' public demands. Google agreed to change its policy that kept claims of harassment out of the courts. Many companies quickly followed suit, and within a year, the California legislature passed a bill to outlaw forced arbitration altogether. The company's response to a highly visible case of sexual harassment was a powerful trigger, but employee activism quickly grew to embrace other issues and concerns.

Googlers take the company founders' ethic of "don't do evil" to heart. Employees began speaking out on business arrangements—perceived acquiescence to censorship in China, contracts with the military, and the treatment of contract workers. By the close of 2019, the company was blocking use of the calendar for organizing large-scale meetings and had begun to rethink all-hands meetings. The media reported that the company even consulted with a firm known for fighting unionization.

The #MeToo movement and #GoogleWalkout offer compelling case examples of the impact of social media and growth in employee social networks. The ease of direct employee-to-employee communication enabled by Slack channels, Google Docs, and Zoom meetings enables teamwork but also has democratized the workforce. Employees schooled in a culture of "move fast and break things" have greater agency, and social networks can also offer anonymity and safety in numbers.

Google employees, led by a small cohort of women, were the first to organize, but segments of the workforce at Microsoft, Amazon, and Wayfair followed suit, challenging specific contracts and actions—or the lack thereof.

Amazon employees first questioned the sale of facial recognition technology to law enforcement and immigration and customs officials. Amazon heard again from employees on working conditions in a Minnesota warehouse and on unpopular elements of a new compensation system. In 2019, when a network called Amazon Employees for Climate Justice challenged CEO Jeff Bezos and the Board of Directors to take aggressive action on climate, they used their own shares to put the issue before the shareholders and make their cause more visible. A six-point plan was signed by more than 8,000 employees.

The company cofounded the Climate Pledge to meet the Paris targets a decade earlier, but employees upped the ante, tying

@AMZNforClimate to the issues of the day, racial equity, and climate justice, and employing every media tool available. In June 2020, the company took further action, creating a $2 billion fund to support the development of technologies and services to reduce carbon emissions. The give and take is likely to continue.

These examples, and many more like them, validate employees as a force to reckon with on an array of concerns that span work, community, and planet.

The issues on the table raise questions about the human condition. The choices that business makes in each case are instrumental. Employees simply, directly, mirror public opinion; on a host of issues—climate change, immigration, human rights, and the challenge of rethinking the business model to embed the environmental principles of the circular economy—the employees are warning shots on complex problems that put corporate reputation and the license to operate at risk.

For Boeing, Wells Fargo, Facebook, and VW, among others, the license to operate was already questioned or revoked. The path back is a long and painful one. If it's a bridge too far for companies to count the activist employees as a blessing, at least they might welcome this window into risks that, if ignored, rebound to the firm.

WHEN EMPLOYEES ASK THE MOST PROVOCATIVE QUESTIONS

One of the demands of the organizers of #GoogleWalkout was to add an employee to the Board of Directors. While Google executives acceded to several demands of the protesters, it did not agree to this one. At least not yet.

US governance norms reject breaking down the walls between management and labor or find doing so impractical in execution. To offer one or more employees a seat on the board defies conventions about director independence and shareholder power and may make some board conversations more difficult.

Of course, creating a seat or two for employees on the board is a lot like requiring at least one woman or a person of color; it does little to change culture and often reinforces stereotypes when that sole voice is expected to represent a segment of the population or way of thinking.

Yet, employee representation on boards is commonplace in highly successful European economies. In both Germany and throughout Scandinavia, corporations are expected to serve the public interest, and the concept of *codetermination*—making room for voices besides those of the shareholders, specifically employees—has survived several rounds of reform of German corporate governance practices. Employee representation on boards is backed by both research and public opinion.

In Germany, the role of employees in governance is a fact of life, even if it is not embraced by everyone. In large companies, half of the seats on the supervisory or oversight board are reserved for employees. The supervisory board in turn appoints the *Vorstand* or managing board. John Bowman, a political scientist who writes about different models of governance in his book *Capitalisms Compared: Welfare, Work, and Business*, reports that in Germany, employee representation is understood as a healthy counterbalance to the short-term interests of shareholders and is considered good for long-term planning and labor relations.[5]

The resistance in the United States to employees' playing a role in governance and policy setting may be a holdover from the contentious culture of labor versus management that defined rapid growth in industrialization in the early 1900s, the trust-busting era of Teddy Roosevelt. It may be time to take a fresh look at the potential of engaging employees in new ways.

Employees have an affinity for the complex relationship between the company and its ecosystem of dependent relationships. They break down the walls between business and society and identify with issues that put the enterprise at risk. When the health of the commons lies in the balance, is there much risk putting your best ally next to you in the driver's seat? Business as usual is not an option. What is possible now?

RESTORING TRUST IN BUSINESS

In October 2019, 250 Facebook employees publicly posted a message to CEO Mark Zuckerberg. The letter challenged the assumption that the company was right to protect political advertising as "free speech" and called for tougher standards—a radical change in business as usual.

The communication from the employees opened another chapter in a story that may play out for years as the social media giant tests the limits of how it utilizes, and sells, personal data. The story is a demoralizing tale of how Facebook executives ignored, tried to hide, and then misrepresented Russia's use of the popular social media site to influence the 2016 US presidential election. With the revenue model of paid advertising at risk, everyone but a few whistleblowers remained silent. It was employees who eventually challenged the leadership to stop taking political ads until protocols to determine veracity could be established.

If anyone in the disheartening story can be called heroes, it's not the executives with the most influence, access, and power. It's the employees who witnessed malfeasance and bypassed protocols to bring it to the highest levels of the company but were ignored or told to look the other way. The proposal to drop all political ads was considered a critical step forward in a complicated give and take between business profits and societal well-being. It was the employees who identified protocols to restore trust—and morale.

◆ ◆ ◆

As Boeing's fiasco with the 737 Max makes clear, sometimes embracing rather than rejecting superior knowledge of employees can be a matter of life and death.

No one has a better or more consistent view of both immediate and long-term effects of management decisions, inside and outside the gate. Employees are now wired for action, have the relevant social networks to amplify their voice, and, as recent examples demonstrate, will no longer stay silent.

The rules and protocols for a new era of employee engagement have not yet emerged. But clear alignment between the workers' desire for economic security and the financial health and long-term reputation of the employer is ripe with opportunity. It's what makes workers so powerful.

Who cares more about the reputation of the company than its employees? *No one.* Who knows more about the conduct of bad actors who can bring harm? Who is the most trusted agent when it comes to assessing the efficiency of the machinery, where to tighten the pipe to reduce emissions, or how to structure work to facilitate childcare and other demands that enable employees to show up ready to work? *The employees.* Employees are in a unique position to connect the inside and the outside—business and the health of the commons.

Real value is created when employees are encouraged to identify and act on long-term risks to the enterprise. We are all better off when employees are productively engaged in what business does at its best: create useful products and services that respect the constraints of nature and individual and community welfare, and secure the brand by ensuring that the company aligns its intentions and actions.

An example of a company that supports the value creators on the front lines of the business is Levi Strauss. CEO Chip Bergh and his team employ a formula that keeps the company on the cutting edge of innovation: values stated must connect firmly with values employed. It's not the cheapest way to operate, but the rewards of doing so are clear. And when you define and design your product with the health of workers and the planet in mind, talent will beat a path to your door.

INNOVATION AND THE QUEST FOR TALENT

The First Movers Fellowship is the brainchild of my longtime colleague Nancy McGaw. It supports innovators working at the intersection of business and society across a swath of industries: *intrapreneurs* working on protocols to support data privacy at MasterCard, growing toxin-free strawberries at Danone, the separation of organic waste from the landfill at Waste Management, ensuring that customers of AT&T have the know-how to keep their kids safe when they acquire their first cell phone.

At Levi Strauss, internal change agents have been free to tackle a host of complex problems—like eliminating toxins from the process of treating denim, creating the "waterless" jean, rewarding best-in-class practices in factories from Mexico to Asia, and leading an industry campaign for sustainable practices in growing cotton. The company also demonstrated first-mover instincts when it chose to publicize the locations of its factories, inviting outside-in accountability.

Chip Bergh joined the company in 2011; he led the turnaround of Levi's and burnished the brand. He has also leaned in on issues like gun control that lie outside the day-to-day concerns of building the business but loom large in the public sphere. This is the kind of company that young people dream about joining—one where your aspirations connect to your paycheck.

For three decades, Levi Strauss was a private company, able to invest in product research, brand building, and efficiency. The company went public in 2019. The founding family still has a controlling interest, and Levi's has been at this rodeo before—it was a public company from 1971 to 1985. The future will tell what demands emerge in a public market that still values return to shareholders over long-term investments, labor, and environmental risks. The decision to furlough workers while continuing to pay a dividend to shareholders in 2020 in the middle of the COVID-19 business meltdown could suggest strong pressure to support the stock price.

Everyone has a role to play; consumers and investors who align their money and their values are critical actors in a system that still rewards short-term thinking and amplifies shareholder pressure. Yet the role of employees is unique. Employees demonstrate a keen understanding of real value creation. It's the employees who have the best line of sight and command of the most useful tools to support the company when conflicts arise.

And why *do* we give so much power to shareholders? In the next chapter, we will examine the conundrum of high returns to shareholders in an era of low demands for capital.

◆ OLD RULE ◆

Capital is king; shareholders rule.

Financial capital is the scarce resource in a hard-asset world; the company is accountable to the shareholders, who "own" the company.

◆ NEW RULE ◆

Culture is king and talent rules.

Value creation emerges from the culture of the enterprise. The CEO embraces diverse talent and teamwork and focuses on key relationships; competitive advantage is attained through superior customer service, human-centered design, and business models in sync with planetary limits.

CHAPTER FIVE

When Capital Is No Longer Scarce

RULE #5

Culture Is King and Talent Rules

I find it useful to keep antique ideas around, as a reminder that how we see things today is not how the world will always see them.

—MARJORIE KELLY, *THE DIVINE RIGHT OF CAPITAL*

I WAS LISTENING to a presentation for new authors on how to market your book when someone made a clever suggestion: Take a photo of a pile of books that have influenced you, write a post about why each was important, and tag the authors to enlist their marketing help.

I quickly made up my list in my head. Lynn Stout's book *The Shareholder Value Myth* was one; and works of Chip and Dan Heath, especially *Switch: How to Change Things When Change Is Hard*, would be on the pile. I recalled how Margaret Blair's book *Ownership and Control: Rethinking Corporate Governance for the Twenty-First Century* practically leapt off the shelf of the bookstore in the lobby of the Brookings Institution, where I met Margaret during her fellowship there. I would also want to include Roger Martin's *Fixing the Game*. But the top of the pile belongs to Marjorie Kelly, who published *The Divine Right of Capital: Dethroning the Corporate Aristocracy* in 2001, just as I was beginning to convene executives in dialogue about the role and purpose of the corporation.

They say that you can get most business books in the first 30 pages. In this case, I felt like I got my money's worth in the opening paragraphs, in which Kelly asks, "Stockholders fund major public corporations—true or false?" and then answers her own question: "*False. Or . . . a tiny bit true—but for the most part, massively false.*"[1]

Marjorie proceeds to dissect how public markets work and to remind us that the company receives its money at the initial public offering (IPO). That capital is used to invest in the business, as needed, and when times are good, the company pays a dividend to the shareholders of record. The stock market offers liquidity—the ability to buy and sell shares at will—and dividends, or returns to traders and investors, including individuals and institutions, such as pension funds, endowments, and other funds that invest on behalf of individuals. But after the original capital raising, for the company itself the public markets are of no direct importance. The company doesn't benefit if the stock price goes up, nor is it directly affected if the stock goes down.

Most public companies don't return to public markets to raise additional capital. Today, they do distribute most of the earnings to public shareholders, however, and in recent decades the distribution has exceeded 90 percent of profits. Some of the distribution, roughly 45 percent, is made through paying regular dividends. But most of it happens through the repurchase of shares at their market or trading value, so-called share buybacks. When the company buys up shares, typically they are then retired, which boosts the value of the outstanding shares of stock by simply reducing the number of shares outstanding.

As management gurus remind us, the most important assets of the company go home at night—or now, even work *from* home. Growth may not require any capital investment at all. For two companies we will consider in this chapter, access to the public markets made it easier for early investors to liquidate their shares, but no additional capital was raised for the company by going public.

Financial capital is no longer a scarce resource. Access to credit and equity investment is no longer as important a consideration as it was when the United States was growing as an industrial power with tremendous need of capital investment in plants and equipment and infrastructure. The decision rules that dominate finance classes—the capital asset pricing model and discounted cash flow—were designed for a different era. Success today is about culture—building and leveraging talent and the stewardship of relationships and nature.

Why do we assign capital markets so much power?

Marjorie Kelly wrote *The Divine Right of Capital* after years of publishing *Business Ethics* magazine, a readable digest of stories about corporate social responsibility. After years of studying businesses, Marjorie wanted more. She began to question fundamentals about how the corporation is created—what is it designed to *do*? Her subsequent books have explored the idea that *ownership* is key—the "original systems condition"—how intentions are first set and are sustained.

Marjorie was among the first to challenge the preeminence of the stock market, the idea that "capital is king." *The Divine Right of Capital* was published as the implosion of Enron reverberated in the markets and demonstrated what is at risk when the return to shareholders becomes the central preoccupation of the company. Marjorie not only upends the importance of the shareholder but makes a fair case that someone who holds the stock today is the least important, not the most important, of its constituents.

Highly respected business managers prove her case.

General Robert Wood Johnson, son of the founder of Johnson & Johnson, authored the company's famous Credo in 1943, while the country was just emerging from the Great Depression. When I visited company headquarters in New Brunswick, New Jersey, I was pleasantly surprised to find that the Credo I had heard so much about is literally carved in a massive piece of stone that dominates the lobby of the main entrance. One assumes that it was placed there as a testament to the founding values—but maybe also as a warning to future generations that you can't just paint the Credo over.

When I reread the Credo in 2020, it seemed like it could have been written yesterday.

The opening line is "We believe our first responsibility is to the patients, doctors and nurses, to mothers and fathers and all others who use our products and services." It references quality and good service and the need for business partners to earn a "fair profit." The next paragraph talks about respect for and dignity of employees and the importance of a "fair wage"; it says that employees need support in their responsibilities to family and should "feel free to make suggestions and complaints." The third paragraph is about the importance of the communities where J&J works.

The Credo concludes with this statement:

> Our final responsibility is to our stockholders. Business must make a sound profit. We must experiment with new ideas. Research must be carried on, innovative programs developed, investments made for the future and mistakes paid for. New equipment must be purchased, new facilities provided and new products launched. Reserves must be created to provide for adverse times. When we operate according to these principles, the stockholders should realize a fair return.

Jim Burke was CEO of J&J from 1976 to 1989. In 1982, he managed through the crisis that ensued when seven people died in the Chicago area from ingesting Tylenol capsules laced with cyanide. Burke's deft management of the situation, including the immediate recall of all the product sold, and how he took responsibility for the problem, became the gold standard for protecting a company's reputation in crisis.

When I interviewed Burke a decade after he left the company, he spoke about the Credo as a living document. The values articulated, especially putting the patient first, meant his team knew exactly what to do in the moment. As a result, the damage to the Tylenol brand, to J&J, and to the stock price proved temporary.

Marjorie Kelly's great contribution to the management literature links decision-making to *corporate design*. A decade later, in his provocative book *Fixing the Game: Bubbles, Crashes, and What Capitalism Can Learn from the NFL*, Roger Martin explored the logic of paying executives in stock.

Given the real function of the stock market, an after-market with strong currents of speculative and even algorithmic trading, how do you resolve the conflicts inherent in rewarding the executive in shares of stock? Can you sustain a customer-first or employee-centric culture if the chief executive is being paid first and foremost to align his or her goals with the shareholders—i.e., to maximize the stock price? (We will return to this question in chapter 7.)

WHAT IS THE PURPOSE OF PUBLIC CAPITAL MARKETS?

Capital markets today bring fresh examples to the narrative that now questions the shareholder-centric thinking that dominated the last three decades.

Spotify, the innovative music streaming program that fully disrupted conventions for listening to popular music, is Exhibit A. In 2018, the company, which was founded in Sweden but then moved its headquarters to the UK, "went public" in name only, eschewing the usual fanfare of ringing the opening bell at the NYSE and most of the conventions of an IPO.

The trading price of Spotify stock exceeded expectations in the early hours of trading—the customary measure of success—but the CEO had already made clear his real goal: a direct listing to match public buyers with private sellers. There was no investment bank in the mix to bolster the stock price as needed; in fact, capital raising for the company itself wasn't the goal. Achieving a high price was nice for the sellers, but it wasn't all that material for the company.

The day before the public listing, cofounder Daniel Ek spoke to the company's goals:

> Spotify is not raising capital, and our shareholders and employees have been free to buy and sell our stock for years. So, while tomorrow puts us on a bigger stage, it doesn't change who we are, what we are about, or how we operate.
>
> Normally, companies ring bells. Normally, companies spend their day doing interviews on the trading floor touting why their stock is a good investment. Normally, companies don't pursue a direct listing. While I appreciate that this path makes sense for most, Spotify has never been a normal kind of company. . . . Our focus isn't on the initial splash. Instead, we will be working on trying to build, plan, and imagine for the long term.[2]

This trend has been in the works for a long time, evidenced by the scholarship of individuals like Jerry Davis—an Aspen Ideas Worth Teaching Award winner from the Ross School of Business at the University of Michigan—who uses market data to point out that providers of financial capital are the least critical part of the stakeholder management matrix.

Data from Jerry's book *The Vanishing Corporation: Navigating the Hazards of a New Economy* shows that the number of public companies declined by nearly one-half in the first decade of the 2000s. Jerry mines the deep decline in the number of publicly listed stocks to better understand performance of the stock market and our day-to-day reality and experience in the economy.

Financial capital is still important. Entrepreneurs still need venture money to get their companies off the ground, and value investors can support them through stages of growth, but overall, we are witnessing significant shifts in the purpose of capital markets.

PERFORMANCE IN THE STOCK MARKET VS. THE HEALTH OF THE REAL ECONOMY

A recent example makes the case. The stock market was turbulent as the consequences of COVID-19 became manifest in early spring 2020 but then began to climb again, even as a growing number of retailers declared bankruptcy, unemployment climbed to numbers last seen in the Great Depression, and Main Street businesses sent warnings about slow-to-no recovery after the crisis. Signs of a rocky economic future are abundant. The connection between the economic health of the nation and the performance of the stock market seem tenuous or nonexistent.

One theory about the disconnect has to do with the performance of a handful of companies. Facebook, Apple, Amazon, Alphabet, and Microsoft represent close to 20 percent of the overall market capitalization. The belief that they are not likely to lose ground in the pandemic—and could even gain market share—might explain the health of the market overall.

My colleague, Miguel Padró, explores a second rationale for the disconnect between a rising stock market and the health of the economy overall. The vast holdings in the market are highly concentrated; 1 percent of investors hold roughly 40 percent of the market value overall (the top 10 percent account for 80 percent of market holdings) and are protected from the severe economic dislocations felt by most Americans. The market may be a bellwether, but only for a tiny, wealthy core, which is also overwhelmingly white. More than 60 percent of white households own stock; only 30 percent of Black and Hispanic households do. The proportion of the stock market held by Black and Hispanic college graduates is under 3 percent.[3]

As observers of the stock market scratched their heads over the growing disconnect, Jerry was quick to tweet out a May 2020 article in the *New York Times* by Matt Phillips titled "Repeat After Me: The Markets Are Not the Economy."

So why do public capital markets have so much sway?

Part of the answer is embedded in old, sticky ideas and habits from a time when access to publicly traded capital mattered a lot. At its peak, General Motors had one million employees on its payroll, all in the United States. The ongoing need for capital to invest in both facilities and labor was a driving concern of management.

UK economist John Kay writes about capital markets. I went to visit him after he was commissioned by the British government to study the causes of the financial market meltdown in 2008. In addition to reporting on the short-term behavior of market makers, he spoke about a widening gulf between equity markets and their original purpose: providing companies with growth capital and giving small investors and savers a piece of the economic pie.

At the conference of the Inclusive Capitalism Coalition in London in 2018, Kay asserted that the dual purpose of providing capital for growth and linking savers to the economic engine "has been forgotten."

Kay is an economist, but also a business historian. He took us through the changes in business over the last 200-plus years, from the time when the Lloyds still owned Lloyds Bank and John and Benjamin Cadbury established the Cadbury Brothers chocolate factory, and then on to the turn of the last century when wealth-building financiers like J. P. Morgan and Henry Clay Frick stood behind John D. Rockefeller of Standard Oil, Andrew Carnegie and his steel factories, and Cornelius Vanderbilt and the railroads.

He also reminded us of the remarkable growth in business and wealth made possible by the creation of joint-stock companies that attracted new shareholders with the protection of limited liability. With professional managers and almost unlimited access to capital, family businesses like DuPont and Johnson & Johnson grew into global enterprises.

Kay fast-forwarded to the reality today that most financial capital is invested and managed by a set of intermediaries who have little or nothing to do with the actual management of the business. They are investing other people's money and sit at a remove from the classic Ma and Pa investor. Many, even most of us in the market, are not able to say which stocks we own.

Today, the companies at the top of the market capitalization tables represent a different breed of enterprise with a different relationship to capital. If Apple, Microsoft, and Amazon are in a tug of war over who has the greatest market value, it is not clear why—it matters little to the companies themselves. John Kay uses Apple as a typical example of a fast-moving business of today: manufacturing is contracted out to a remote supplier, there are few hard assets, and there is a full-time global labor force of only 123,000—not that many, given the company's market reach and influence. Kay continued,

> And what of Apple's $800 billion [$1.4 trillion in early 2020] market capitalization? So wedded are we to the idea that capital is critical to business, so much in thrall to the word, that we have invented new concepts such as social and intellectual capital to try to explain phenomena that are perhaps more clearly and certainly more simply described in ordinary language.[4]

Public markets offer an exit for venture capitalists and early-round investors, as in the case of Spotify, but the need for fresh capital to invest is modest to nonexistent. The evidence is the piles of cash on Apple's balance sheet.

The disconnect between the role of the stock market and the path to value creation is also understood through how stock-based voting power is assigned today. When Snapchat, the photo and video sharing app, went public in 2017, it went even further than Google, Facebook, and LinkedIn, whose dual-class shares diluted the voting power of the common shareholders. Snapchat thumbed its nose at public market norms and offered *no voting rights at all.*

Snapchat's decision was a radical departure from the norms of shareholder value, but it is a perfectly legal, and honest—if extreme—signal of how the company thinks about risks borne and the responsibilities of shareholders. Snapchat and Spotify may raise the hackles of some investors, but the founders are also acting rationally. Financial capital is no longer a scarce resource. Why grant it so much power?

Should we be concerned about these trends? Not according to Kay, who talks about the advent of the "hollow" corporation: few employees, little need for capital, basically a set of relationships and codependencies.

It is useful to recall a key tenet of *The Shareholder Value Myth* by Lynn Stout: *The only thing shareholders own is the stock certificate itself.* Shareholders still make waves, but they are no longer the powerful accountability mechanism or arbiter of real value creation that the myths about public markets would have us believe.

In order to understand the drivers of innovation and competitive advantage, the contributors to real value, we need to turn to other aspects of the business model—specifically, the culture of the enterprise and the clarity of intentions, rewards, execution, and accountability mechanisms that shape business decisions.

Deep changes in business culture are underway. The ability to attract and keep the best talent is critically important in growth sectors dependent on innovation and technology. The stability of the supply chain is another complicated management task for consumer goods and B2B suppliers. CEOs need the emotional intelligence that might be better associated with managing a complex social institution. For public companies, when the leadership succeeds at managing teams and relationships in this environment, a robust stock price should follow—it is no longer the organizing principle for decision-making.

CAPITAL MARKETS AND CORPORATE PURPOSE

Larry Fink's 2019 letter to the CEOs of BlackRock's portfolio companies landed at a moment that felt economically rocky and socially perilous in Washington, London, Paris, and around the globe—as he described it, a time of popular anger, nationalism, and xenophobia.

He reminded business leaders, even those beset by quarterly expectations and the drumbeat of investors focused on share price, that their
job had changed.

This moment required more from business leaders.

Fink posed a fundamental question: What might be possible if
a company sets a direction that prioritizes social value—defines its
public purpose—and then truly lives by it?

Fink's platform and influence comes from overseeing the largest
pool of capital on the globe, $7 trillion in assets under management
in 2020. He continues to speak out forcefully on the public purpose of
the enterprise. And his message is authentic; it makes sense against
BlackRock's own business model.

BlackRock is an asset manager with an array of products, but for
the most part it is known as a massive index fund. Rather than moving in and out of stocks to capture upside gains and minimize losses,
most of BlackRock's assets are managed for small investors following
the advice of financial gurus like Warren Buffett or John Bogle, the
founder of Vanguard: over the long haul, you are better off betting on
the market overall than paying someone hefty fees to try to beat the
market by picking stocks. These individual savers, and the pensions
that invest on their behalf, place money in an index fund to mirror the
market, or a representative sample of the market, like the S&P 500 or
Dow Jones Industrial Average.

Like its competitors, Vanguard and Fidelity, BlackRock owns a
piece—a significant piece—of every public company. Index funds like
BlackRock are also called *universal* investors; their success is tied to
the health of the market overall, not the give and take of individual
stocks. They can't exit a stock without undermining the basic concept
of investing in the index, and thus BlackRock has a keen interest in
good management—and a healthy economic ecosystem over the long
haul.

Like Larry Fink, Bill McNabb, chairman of Vanguard, advises
executives to allocate capital in a way that builds for the long term.

The conditions for economic health, and planetary health, are critical to Vanguard's own vitality and near-infinite investor horizons.

How do you manage when the scale of the assets under management requires you to hold everything? How do you respond to the impulses of small investors on dicey issues like guns and labor conditions and climate, when your business model means that you can never dump a stock?

Welcome to the conundrum of the world's largest investors. More like the world's largest stock-sitters. Even with the financial power of a BlackRock or Vanguard, the influence of our largest investors in the public markets is significant but limited in scope. At critical moments, such as in a takeover challenge from an activist investor, their voting power is supremely important. Yet, with higher proportions of the assets in the stock market invested through index funds, we are experiencing another aspect of the decline of financial capital as the organizing principle of decision-making.

Fink believes in the markets, but he lives with their limitations. He commands the attention of company executives because BlackRock is typically their largest investor. Rather than issuing threats, BlackRock's real influence is derived by prodding CEOs to be good stewards of their companies—i.e., through strategic, disciplined, long-term management of tens of thousands, or even hundreds of thousands, of employees and through suppliers and brands.

DEFINING CULTURE

I don't know how Larry Fink and Bill McNabb respond when asked for specific examples of companies that live up to their vision of purposeful business. As the world's largest investors, they may need to dodge the question. When I am asked for the names of companies that take business purpose seriously—a question that used to begin with "Who do you have besides Unilever?"—I answer with half a dozen public and private companies that have been so consistent at living by long-term, employee- and customer-centric values, they almost fade from view.

Southwest Airlines, whose cofounder and long-time CEO, Herb Kelleher, passed away in 2018, is always on the list. Kelleher placed both employees (profit-sharing, respect, dignity) and customers (low fares, clean planes, "no stupid fees") at the center of decisions. The investors who stuck around for the ride were handsomely rewarded. Kelleher managed the most financially successful US airline in history, and Southwest is a textbook case for whether high-road employment practices can earn a decent, or even superior, ROI.

With a 45-year track record, Southwest illustrates beautifully Fink's call for a long-term plan and his conjecture that profits are not only consistent with purpose but inextricably linked.

The culture is defined by the allocation of capital and the operational protocols. For Southwest, a focus on employees is instrumental to the business model and long-term success. A superb customer experience is a by-product of the focus on employees. Service protocols are the airline's equivalent of quality control on a factory floor. Good service requires walking in the shoes of others and caring about everyone who influences the customer's experience.

Kelleher could have written these words at the end of the J&J Credo: *When we operate according to these principles, the stockholders should realize a fair return.*

Herman Miller is another example of a defining culture that becomes the organizing principle for value creation.

The company, known for the Aeron chair and for introducing modern furniture design to American households, opened its doors as the Star Furniture Company in Zeeland, Michigan, in 1905. D. J. De Pree began working there as a clerk in 1909 and purchased the company in 1923 with the help of his father-in-law, Herman Miller. D. J. stayed at the helm until 1969. Many of the decisions he made, including his support for design innovation and the introduction of an employee stock plan, had a lasting effect.

The culture of Herman Miller tightly weaves together respect for the talents of people who work at the company and the impact of the products they make. In the words of De Pree, "In the long run, all businesses and business leaders will be judged not by their profits or their products but by their impact on *humanity*."

Dozens of books have been written about the designers that Herman Miller supported and the modern design aesthetic it embedded in our world, but also about the culture instituted by its founder. *Leadership Is an Art*, by Max De Pree, D.J.'s son, is a classic of management literature; it was Bill Clinton's bible on leadership. Max helped lead the company beginning in the 1960s, supporting the company's growth by instilling a culture of inclusiveness and design innovation.

The company didn't formalize its purpose statement until recently—it didn't need to; the purpose was baked in: "At Herman Miller, we respect each other as we are, and who we will become. Our culture represents our collective attitudes, aspirations, ideas and experience of the people who work here."

The bottom-up culture is evident in early and unstinting support for design talent, beginning with Gilbert Rohde—who was recruited by D.J. in 1930 and introduced the modern aesthetic and the first line of office furniture for which the company is known—and including George Nelson, Charles and Ray Eames, Isamu Noguchi, and a who's-who list of design masters who have collaborated with Herman Miller through the last century to create classic industrial design.

Trusting the aspirations of your people and diversity of thinking go hand in hand. A culture based on respect enables cutting-edge thinking to take root. The ideas that emerged in this environment still shape the culture of today, from attention to quality ("reliability") and human-centered design to sustainability. Bill Birchard's book *Merchants of Virtue: Herman Miller and the Making of a Sustainable Company* tells how Herman Miller's unique culture allowed the principles of environmental sustainability to emerge from its employees early on in the 1990s; the company still leads its industry on sustainability in design and architecture.

Herman Miller is a public company; former CEO Brian Walker talked about the company's fiduciary duty to shareholders as a moral

---

When Intentions and Operations Collide

In the early 2000s, when we began the Business Leaders Dialogue, the Aspen Institute's campus in Colorado was managed by the Aspen Skiing Company and the hotel rooms bore the now-ubiquitous signs that instruct the guest to be mindful of the beautiful surroundings and precious natural resources of the Rocky Mountains:

SAVE OUR PLANET

Dear Guest, everyday millions of gallons of water
are used to wash towels that are only used once.

YOU MAKE THE DIFFERENCE

- A towel hanging up means "I will use again."
- A towel on the floor means "Please wash."

Thanks for Helping Us Conserve the Earth's Natural Resources.

An executive reported to the participants in our dialogue that he dutifully hung up his towel each morning after showering. And, every day the housekeeper replaced the towel with a fresh one.

He offered up this seemingly mundane experience as an example of the challenges of driving sustainability through the complex operations of any enterprise, from the good intentions of the chief sustainability officer to the front lines, or into the functional bureaucracy or professional networks that make up the bones of the organization. Where was the breakdown in communications? What was needed to ensure that the good intentions were fulfilled—albeit a goal that also offered cost savings to the corporation?

---

obligation. Investors, he said, entrust their money to the company for a return. Public companies like Herman Miller need to cultivate their shareholders—especially the long-term investors that are critical for support when activist raiders come calling. Long-term investors understand the external pressures and trends that affecperformance, as well as the interplay of a resilient culture and the ability to stay competitive. The priority that Southwest and Herman Miller place on the human element is instrumental.

Consider Delta's remarkable profit-sharing plan, created to appease pilots and flight attendants forced to take severe pay cuts when the company went into bankruptcy in 2005. Every employee of Delta, from the ground crew and gate attendants to the pilots and office workers, receives a check on Valentine's Day representing a proportionate share of profits. In 2019, the year before COVID-19 wiped out the airline industry, the total distribution was $1.3 billion; for five years running, the number had exceeded $1 billion. For many Delta employees, the distribution approximated 14 percent of their salary.

CEO Ed Bastian describes the program as the foundation of a partnership—enabling a culture change and remarkable turnaround by the company. Delta has moved from strength to strength and today enjoys a superior reputation for everything from customer service to on-time arrivals—challenging Southwest at its own game.

What about the culture and priorities of New Economy companies?

One of the values featured in Salesforce's mission statement runs against the grain of winner-take-all-style capitalism: *equality*. CEO Marc Benioff became curious about whether the company was achieving pay equity in its own ranks. The data was clarifying; a one-time investment was made to level up lagging pay for women and to close the gaps within pay grades. Annual assessments ensure that the equity standard is maintained.

The CEO of Microsoft, Satya Nadella, has become the most highly regarded chief executive in the country. He led a transformation of the company's strategy but also its culture—breaking down silos, embracing collaboration, talking about the need for empathy and positive reinforcement, and thinking differently about everything from data standards to open-source technology to the company's relationship with its home base of Seattle and the Puget Sound.

As Microsoft moved back to the top of the list of companies by market capitalization, it announced a $500 million investment to reverse the housing shortage and address homelessness in Seattle. Then, early in 2020, it pledged to not only radically reduce emissions but also invest heavily in carbon capture, in order to draw down from the atmosphere as much carbon as it has released since the company began operating and share the technological solutions with others. These moves reflect a culture that is concerned with the company's contribution to the health of society. Microsoft flourishes in the embrace of both bottom-up and outside-in thinking.

When Royal Dutch Shell articulated clear intentions to achieve net-zero carbon emissions by 2050, it signaled a profound shift in culture. Because it is the largest energy company globally, these goals are particularly meaningful; they require radical change in the company's footprint and operations and are even carried into the executive pay plan. Given the scope of their intentions, Shell will need to work with its customers to embrace the same goals.

TO WHOM DO EXECUTIVES LISTEN NOW?

Even with enlightened leaders, companies with public shareholders manage on a tightrope; they stay attuned to the noisy demands of the short-term investors and outright threats of some, while prioritizing the strategic investments needed to create value for those who are in for the long haul.

Larry Fink promises that BlackRock will back up companies that articulate their public purpose and then live by it—e.g., offer a fair wage for employees and contractors, and engage principles of management that allow the environment and the communities on which the business depends to thrive.

Corporate responsibility, sustainability, consumer trust—none of these are an end state. As with the pursuit of quality or excellence, it is a continuous journey. The path forward is complicated, especially in a company as complex as a Johnson & Johnson or Pepsi or Shell or Microsoft, even if the CEO seems supportive and the culture is conducive.

Within weeks of Microsoft's announcements of bold commitments to address climate change and homelessness, ProPublica, an organization committed to high-quality, long-form journalism, released an exposé on Microsoft. The focus of the article was a decade-long program of tax avoidance. The article described complex negotiations involving the company's tax adviser, KPMG; the IRS; and a Puerto Rican entity that the company engaged to transfer significant commercial value from a high-tax jurisdiction to one with low, or almost no, tax. The story reveals a lot about the murky domain of "transfer pricing" but also the underlying instincts and status quo thinking that persists in the best of companies, and the need for more integrative thinking at the highest levels of the enterprise.

The best leaders, including Satya Nadella of Microsoft and Ben van Beurden of Royal Dutch Shell, are on a journey—one that is not always clearly marked but is seen in the kinds of questions they ask, whom they listen to, how they spend their time, and the beliefs that guide their decisions and investments.

Southwest's CEO, Herb Kelleher, wasn't trying to save the world or "elevate the world's consciousness" like WeWork's colorful founder, Adam Neumann. Kelleher conducted his business with a simple purpose: to make flying affordable for the masses and fun for the crew. In doing so, he transformed an industry and improved the experience of his customers and the lives of his employees.

Microsoft is capable of doing the same and is demonstrating the interest and the staying power we need to tackle remarkably complex problems. As we will see in the next chapter, to make material change when a system is at risk requires a combination of leadership and willingness to collaborate and co-create with competitors—including government in the important role it has to play in setting the rules for fair competition.

In the nomenclature of sports, a healthy corporation is *fit*. Much like an elite athlete, the trustworthy corporation is never done perfecting its game. Real value creators are vigilant about trends and use goals to drive change and mark progress, but they never stop working to upgrade their skills and performance.

It's about mindset, and about building a culture to embrace and absorb standards that are constantly evolving as the business context and public expectations change. As Indra Nooyi, CEO of Pepsi, was known to say, "The journey will not be easy, but important work never is."

◆ OLD RULE ◆

Compete to win.

Competition drives innovation and growth.

◆ NEW RULE ◆

Co-create to win.

When the system itself is at risk, real value creation requires
enlisting business partners along the supply chain; both NGOs
and competitors with aligned interests become business allies.

CHAPTER SIX

When the System Is at Risk

RULE #6

Co-create to Win

To influence something as complex as overfishing, you need to engage—
and trust—your competitors—and forgo the competitive advantage
that may emerge if you only work to secure your own supply chain.
—JIM CANNON, SUSTAINABLE FISHERIES PARTNERSHIP

AT THE HEART OF New York's Midtown business district lies Bryant Park, the most densely occupied urban park in the world. On a summer day it's tough to snare a seat in this magnificent public space surrounded by gleaming skyscrapers, where office workers on their lunch break mix it up with the tourists heading to the theater district or Herald Square. There you will find music, Wi-Fi, yoga, film screenings, an outdoor lending library, and vendors of all kinds. In the winter, the expansive lawn turns into a skating rink, and a soaring Christmas tree and bustling crafts fair replace the folding chairs.

It was not always like this.

In the summer of 1981, a year into business school, I landed in New York City for an internship with the 42nd Street Development Corporation. This scrappy nonprofit was run by Fred Papert, the advertising executive who, with the help of Jackie Onassis, protected the Beaux Arts masterpiece Grand Central Station from development.

Our office was in the old McGraw-Hill Building—a turquoise-, silver-, and gold-striped Art Deco relic on a seedy West Side block. The Development Corporation shared a floor with the police unit tasked with rooting out derelict activity in Times Square. To the west of us was Theatre Row, a stretch of funky avant-garde theaters that Papert incubated as the anchor tenants of his vision for a renaissance of West 42nd Street. Farther east, past Times Square, lay the New York Public Library, Grand Central Station, and some of the best addresses in New York City, including another example of Art Deco splendor, the Chrysler Building, plus the landmarked modern façade of my future employer, the Ford Foundation.

◆ ◆ ◆

On Fridays I would walk the long blocks of 42nd Street to the steps of the New York Public Library to meet my friend Lynn for a sandwich. From the sidewalk, I would glance up to the inviting green canopy of Bryant Park, the backyard of the library. I never set foot inside the park—not then, nor for quite a few years after I moved permanently to New York to become a banker to clothing manufacturers and importers in the Garment Center close by.

The public park, named for William Cullen Bryant, abolitionist and editor of the *New York Evening Post*, has a remarkable history. It was once a potter's field and also contained the city's water reservoir. In 1853, it was home to the Crystal Palace, which welcomed visitors to the 1853 World's Fair. During the Great Depression, the park hosted a WPA-sponsored outdoor reading room for the unemployed. But by the late 1970s, as the city careened toward bankruptcy, Bryant Park became a tangible symbol of the city's decline—a sanctuary for drug dealers, pimps, and the homeless.

How did Bryant Park evolve from a state of neglect to a jewel of the Midtown business district?

As you delve into the Bryant Park story, it tells volumes about what is involved in making change in a complex system. It requires some-one, or a group of someones, who identify with an issue, clarify what is at stake, and build the right coalition to analyze the problem and develop an action plan. A successful plan is well-resourced and long-term in nature but is also open to modification as experience and circumstances demand.

In this case, the story begins in the 1970s with Brooke Astor, den-izen of New York society and major donor to the Public Library, who, according to lore, was incensed when she was accosted by drug deal-ers on the front steps of *her* library.

The turnaround of Bryant Park took decades. It benefited greatly from the stewardship of a visionary leader and true social entrepre-neur, Dan Biederman, who, with a core of committed allies, worked continuously to keep the work headed in the right direction.

But the transformation of Bryant Park was not due to one event or one person's vision.

There was no silver bullet that contributed and sustained the change—it was more of a fusillade of efforts over time, story by story, pitch by pitch, dollar by dollar, brick by brick. Entirely new funding mechanisms and governance structures were created, and larger forces, such as a general drop in the crime rate and an improving economy, also played an important role.

The Parks Council, which formed in the initial states of cleanup, included prominent New Yorkers such as former advertising execu-tive Fred Papert himself; Andrew Heiskell, the head of Time Inc. who chaired the Board of the New York Public Library; and members of the Rockefeller family. Real estate investors and business tenants in the immediate area were recruited along with representatives from city government and key anchor institutions, like the library itself.

Today, the park is owned by the city but is managed by the non-profit Bryant Park Corporation, which accepts no public money but operates 100 percent for the public benefit. Revenues come from private concessions and assessments paid by the surrounding corporations and property owners, who benefit both directly as users and indirectly as investors in recovered real estate values. The Business Improvement District that was created to engage local property owners became a model for development in other New York neighborhoods and well beyond.

In hindsight, it all seems tailor-made for the result we have now. The bigger concerns of inequality, homelessness, and urban crime are still with us, but that reality should not detract from this singular achievement. Walking by Bryant Park on a summer day in 1981, it was beyond my comprehension that this remarkable urban treasure could emerge from the dust.

I am drawn to the Bryant Park story as a tangible example of what is possible when private business interests and the public interest connect around a complex and dynamic problem.

Dealing with the challenges embedded in a physical space, six square blocks in the middle of a vibrant city, feels more straightforward—more doable—than the daunting changes needed to radically reduce dependence on fossil fuels, or rebuild national infrastructure, or restore a fragile ecosystem, or influence the norms that make it difficult to change how CEOs are paid.

Yet, like the other examples of systems change in this chapter, the turnaround of Bryant Park began with the vision of a small number of fellow travelers, including business leaders with institutional levers and deep networks, a personal stake in success, and a belief that the *public benefit* belonged at the heart of their vision. Each of these examples tells a story of co-creation, of how public needs and private interests intersect to create a sustainable future. There is no other path to systemic change than to work together.

Two inspiring examples take us back to the close of World War II. Both stories link national interests with business and community interests.

In the first story, the change agents are three Americans—Paul G. Hoffman, president of Studebaker Corporation; William Benton, founder of the advertising firm of Benton & Bowles; and Marion B. Folsom, treasurer of Eastman Kodak—who began working together in the summer of 1942 on the need for a massive number of private sector jobs at the conclusion of the war.

They created a new organization called the Committee for Economic Development (CED). The purpose of CED was to guide the transition of business from a war economy to a peacetime economy without falling, again, into recession—or worse. The effort began years before the war ended and it embraced an ambitious agenda, including some mundane but also complex problems, like how to unwind war supply contracts, refocus tax incentives, and plan for postwar production to minimize strains on the system and "set business' own sights for high employment."[1]

The charter of the Committee for Economic Development anticipated the need for 7 to 10 million more jobs than the United States had in 1940, a peak year of peacetime production. The vision was bold. If free enterprise and democracy were to flourish, jobs that offered returning servicemen both dignity and adequate income had to be created at a remarkable pace.

The Economics of a Free Society

In that part of the economy where private enterprise can better serve the common good, the people, through their government, must devise and enforce rules of the game—reasonably stable rules, that will encourage private, voluntary enterprise—rules to which government itself will adhere, and which government will enforce—rules that intelligent and forward-looking men can understand and under which they can operate for the common and for their own good.

—WILLIAM BENTON, BENTON & BOWLES, *FORTUNE*, OCTOBER 1944

This band of brothers set out to enlist national business interests that in turn would ignite local business networks all over the county to begin to plan for the employment needed to absorb the troops as they returned from the front.

We often celebrate US engagement in the execution of the war and the prolonged period of economic expansion that followed, but there is more to the story than public support for infrastructure and higher education and the invisible hand at work.

The track record is impressive. In only a few years' time, the membership of CED grew to 50,000 businessmen across 2,000 communities as the local networks kicked into gear. The leaders of the CED didn't stop there; they also built the political support among business executives for the Marshall Plan to rebuild Europe. In both efforts, the benefits to the business community were rooted in a common sense understanding of the interdependence of business and society.

For the economy to gain strength, and for business to prosper —whether selling Studebakers, washing machines, or advertising— people need jobs and disposable income. The notion of an old boys' network determining the fate of the nation may feel cringeworthy, especially with the benefit of hindsight about the fate of women and people of different races and skin colors, whose contributions to the war effort are legendary but failed to earn them a place in the recovery effort. Yet the sheer scale and pace of job creation to reabsorb millions into the private workforce and avoid a postwar slump is a remarkable achievement. It should be a template for what is required of business and industry and the professions as we work to build an economy that works for all.

THE POWER OF A SMALL GROUP

I have not read an account of how the Hoffman-Benton-Folsom team got started. I don't know who first picked up the phone to call whom or attended the first and later gatherings as the group coalesced around a strategy and put a plan in motion, but I envision the first encounter taking place around a dining room table, not in a conference room. The thinking and envisioning stage required deep trust—colleagues who shared a common view of the future—and commitment to build the network, a network of networks needed to get the job done.

The founders' profound belief in free enterprise permeated their vision for the common good. It is impossible to read the principles under which they operated without thinking about the levels of inequality and financial insecurity that test our public institutions today and undermine trust in both government and the private sector:

> The good of all—the common good—is a means to the enduring happiness of every individual in society and is superior to the economic interest of any private group, not only in war (when the validity of the principle is obvious) but in peace as well. . . . An economic system based on private enterprise, Americans believe, can better serve the common good, not because it enables some men to enrich themselves, but because it develops a high and rapidly rising level of living. . . . It can provide the largest economic opportunity for the largest number of individuals of the community.[2]

These are lofty ideas. Like any vision statement, they take on meaning only as they become concrete and actionable and are sustained over a prolonged period of trial and error, course correction, reenvisioning, and reinvesting—the 99 percent perspiration part of the equation.

GETTING THE RIGHT PEOPLE IN THE ROOM

Another game-changing conversation from the same period of time began after the end of the US occupation of Japan. It started with a dinner party. The guest list included 21 leaders of Japan's most important industries, who were invited to Tokyo in 1950 to meet the American statistician W. Edwards Deming. Deming convinced the dinner guests that a focus on *quality* was the key to reinvigorating the country's economy. Collectively, and without regulation or legislation, these leaders coalesced around Deming's vision, jump-starting a manufacturing renaissance that turned "Made in Japan" into an unbeatable brand of consistently high quality.

It took decades more, and the imprimatur of the US military, for the tenets of Deming's message to take hold in the United States. The practices and protocols embedded in the Quality Movement—or Six Sigma, or Lean Manufacturing—still animate thinking in the C-suite and on the shop floor. A singular focus on the customer, the notion of continuous improvement, and the importance of listening to the workers began to permeate many corners of business, not just manufacturing.

In Japan, *Kaizen*, the "Japanese way," reached a tipping point after a careful period of vetting and trial and error, supported by a group of individual leaders who in a different context might have been competitors but joined the party out of a common need. A fundamental reset was required to increase the value of a critically important common asset, the brand of a nation.

In the United States, the transformation of manufacturing required many supports and assists, just like the turnaround of Bryant Park. For a new way of thinking and the focus on quality to move into the mainstream of a much larger and more complex economy, many structures and institutions emerged: standard-setting bodies and award programs like the Malcolm Baldrige National Quality Award; frameworks like Six Sigma; standard bearers like GE; special-purpose trade associations—all of these played a role in shifting mindsets and capturing the attention of management.

The problem could not be solved by one company or even an industry. The upside benefit of investing in the commons was clear; everyone at the table would benefit from firm-specific investments to change practices across manufacturing. A table of industrial leaders, guiding both private and public investment, was sufficient to negotiate the steps involved.

Who needs to be at the table for the problems we face now? Getting the right people in the room may still be the most important first step—but who is invited to the party when designing for the future creates both winners and losers?

Who are the right people to frame the problem, identify the levers of change, and search for solutions when much greater diversity of experience and networks is required to get the job done? The imagery of a dinner party as a conversation starter works when the host is one or maybe two degrees of separation from the guests—when they would all be at home in the same club.

Who will represent those usually left out of the conversation altogether—who are the most vulnerable and have the most to lose? What mechanisms allow for long-term thinking to take root and to imagine the voices of future generations—those who will bear the consequences of inaction?

The challenges we face now are just as complex as recovering from the Great Depression and transitioning from the war economy were—in significant ways, more so. A cacophony of voices that call for change is hard to hear clearly amid protestations of those who benefit from the status quo. The confusion in the public square, and fears about future consequences of taking action or the prospect of inaction, emerge in the low levels of trust in institutions of all kinds. We, the people, need to discern the common good, but progress is stymied; the voices we hear are discordant.

The moonshot moment on climate; preparing for mass recalibration of work in an era of artificial intelligence; opening up an economy to face economic exclusion, racism, and inequality—a persistent blind spot in our economic evolution—each of these challenges requires business at the table with clarity of purpose and long-term commitment to the health of the commons.

Inaction is not a choice. It's time to pick up the pace of change.

BUILDING TRUST AT THE TABLE—THE COD INDUSTRY

An example of contemporary problem-solving on a systems challenge of remarkable complexity comes out of the cod industry in the Barents

Sea, which spans the arctic shores of Norway and Russia between the North Atlantic and the Arctic Ocean. Once the backbone of the economy in the North Atlantic, cod is a mild-flavored white fish commonly used in fish and chips and fish filet sandwiches. Cod liver oil is still a popular nutritional supplement.

In the 1600s, codfish was so ubiquitous and central to nutrition that it played a starring role in the triangle trade among Europe, Africa, and the Americas. Entire books have been written that chronicle age-old battles about fishing rights and attempts to govern cod fishing on the open seas. Cod was abundant and also lucrative. Dried cod of high quality was shipped from the rocky shoals of New England to as far away as Asia. The slave economy depended on cod from Newfoundland; "salt fish" was an inexpensive, high-protein form of sustenance on the sugar and cotton plantations of the Caribbean.

Today, cod is a threatened species and a symbol of the failure of markets to self-regulate. Regardless of cod's status on the watch lists of environmentalists, it still pays for rogue operators to flout expansive protocols designed to sustain the fish supply for the long term. The threats to productive fisheries in this moment are very real. Newfoundland cod stock declined to such a degree in the early 1990s that even after a long-standing moratorium on fishing, it remains largely depleted and may never recover.

The pressures on the health of cod, haddock, and other fish stocks in the North Atlantic range from climate change to unintended effects of fish farms, but the major factor is what NGO activists label "IUU" catch: "illegal, unregulated, and unreported" fishing. IUU fishing is the underbelly of the high demand for cheap fish for ready markets in the UK, Europe, and North America.

The strategy deployed by groups from WWF to Greenpeace is a familiar one. The fishing industry—including suppliers that encompass everything from industrial-scale trawlers to intermediaries who engage in piracy—is hard to influence and harder to govern. Direct campaigns aimed at the consumption of fish by mass consumers are horribly complicated given the market confusion of varieties, origins, and substitutes. The activists have focused instead on a brand with significant leverage up the supply chain—one that is vulnerable to social media and headlines.

Enter McDonald's.

In 2007, Greenpeace released the following announcement:

> Oslo/Amsterdam, International—Eight of Europe's largest and most influential seafood companies have signed and addressed a joint letter to the Norwegian government, committing to do their best to avoid illegal Barents Sea cod and have called on the Norwegian government to provide up-to-date black lists so companies can live up to this commitment. The signatories include some of Europe's largest seafood processors and purchasers such as restaurant chain McDonald's as well as Espersen, Royal Greenland, Young's Seafood and Iglo/Birds Eye, Frosta/Copack.[3]

The focal point of the campaign is McDonald's, which sources product across the world to feed about 70 million people each day. McDonald's customers are drawn to quality and convenience at an affordable price, and behind the restaurant chain's promise of tasty, well-priced food lies a complex set of suppliers, brokers, and producers that span some of the most environmentally sensitive places on the planet.

The arctic waters of the Barents Sea encompass one of the last healthy fishing grounds for highly popular white fish. The party convened to confront the declining health of these fisheries was led by Klaus Nielsen, CEO of Espersen, a Danish enterprise set up in 1937 for cod fishing in the Baltic Sea.

With 2,500 employees around the globe and an annual turnover of more than 200 million euros, Espersen is today a major supplier of processed white fish. The company's history is chronicled on its website, but its *future* depends on a steady supply of cod:

In the years ahead, we wish to further consolidate our business in order to be able to continue to absorb and learn from the challenges of the world and the market. As such, we steadily continue on the journey we set sails to undertake more than 75 years ago to ensure that we can serve delicious fish to our grandchildren 25 years from now—as well as to many generations to come.[4]

I had a chance meeting with Nielsen and members of the company's industry association, AIPCE, plus Jason Clay of WWF and Jim Cannon, founder of Sustainable Fisheries Partnership, at the Rockefeller Foundation's conference center in Bellagio, Italy. The industry executives who participated in the dialogue depend on a delicate balance of guardrails and protocols to protect fisheries—ideally without killing off current production and revenue.

These producers sell into the vast market for what Americans once called fish sticks, including all forms of processed and breaded white fish that are still highly popular in lunchrooms, as frozen convenience food, and on McDonald's menus throughout the world.

In 2006, the fishing industry in the Barents Sea was in crisis. A Swedish TV show had run a sting operation and released damning film footage that featured traders selling cheap cod from vessels that flouted the region's fishing limits. Local authorities were offering phony or "fig leaf" quotas for illegal catch, and fishery management authorities and Norwegian scientists estimated then that as much as 50 percent of the catch violated negotiated limits.

The public reaction to the story proved a great opportunity for Cannon, whose organization, the Sustainable Fisheries Partnership, acts as a go-between among the private producers, the retailers, and the NGOs working to excise illegal fishing. Cannon was advising both McDonald's and Espersen at the time, and discussions about a response were already underway. Public visibility was the missing link; it offered a platform for the campaigners to tie rogue operators back to the producers—and, ultimately, to the retailers and consumers. Cannon recalled it this way:

Truls Gulowsen—aka Greenpeace Nordic—drew the lines and exposed the connections from the traders to companies like Espersen, and then to McDonald's. Greenpeace originally asked for observers on vessels and full traceability, but the industry resisted; they did not think that would work. It took the public exposure to really get it to the top of the agenda for all the main buyers, to get things moving.[5]

For producers like Espersen who depend on a steady supply of cod and white fish, a sustainable business plan required finding a way to keep the whole supply chain accountable. As the largest producer in the region, Espersen was the linchpin. Like the real estate owners eager to revitalize the park next door, or the Japanese businessmen tied to the brand quality of Made in Japan, regional producers including Espersen have real skin in the game.

McDonald's is Espersen's largest customer. The massive restaurant chain could choose to source elsewhere, and fleets operating in the Barents Sea have some freedom of movement, but the health of the fisheries in the Baltic and Barents Sea region was the lifeblood of Scandinavian and European producers like Espersen. If McDonald's, the most popular restaurant chain in the world, severed its relationship, Espersen's future was at risk.

But CEO Klaus Nielsen could not solve the problem alone. With the help of Jim Cannon's organization, Espersen engaged the main European importers and, ultimately, its trade association to agree to police every vessel in the supply chain, using a contract and protocol that quickly became the industry standard. It heavily penalizes and eventually enforces a boycott on any trader who fails to assure that its catch is legal.

The solution was engineered by industry leaders with the most to lose, thus the most to gain by ratcheting up the operating standard. When leaders raise the bar to protect their operating license, competitors follow.

Cannon explained how the contract works in practice in an email he sent in response to my query about the process:

> The contract basically says, "Cheat me on one shipment and I'll stop buying until you demonstrate you're 100 percent clean, and if I hear you cheated any of my customers, I'll also stop buying. . . . And by the way, if you cheat me, I'm going to alert all my competitors." By this means, a disreputable trader risks losing all their main customers—rather than losing just that catch . . . so it's a much bigger deterrent . . . far bigger than the formal fines.[6]

The program was a huge success. The road to arrive at a solution was a long one, but within six months, the fig leaf quota boats dropped out of the cod fishery, and illegal fishing dropped to near *zero*.

Building trust was critical to the system coalescing around a workable solution—and to the ability to co-create. Cannon continued,

> We worked with the NGOs to ensure they understood and were ok with what the industry was trying to do—and to see that all the parties were aligned, at least privately, if not publicly. The individual relationships built between the businesses and Greenpeace have sustained to this day, which is a huge side benefit.[7]

At this writing, the Barents Sea has since been the world's largest source of sustainable cod—a healthy fishery, certified by the gold standard for sustainable seafood, the Marine Stewardship Council.

Bob Langert retired from McDonald's in 2015. During his 25-year tenure, he managed dozens of complex negotiations between and among the company and the stakeholders representing various interests—including the parties to the agreement to secure the health of the fisheries in the Barents Sea. In 2019, he published *The Battle to Do Good: Inside McDonald's Sustainability Journey*, which chronicles his experience at the center of a host of hot-button issues that defined his time with the company.

As he began sketching out the lessons learned in 2016, Bob accepted our invitation to visit with members of our forum for enterprise-level leaders responsible for sustainability and stakeholder management—Citibank to Johnson & Johnson to Chevron. He had a handwritten list of ideas that he spoke from.

Bob and Jim Cannon agreed on at least three key ingredients for enlisting a critical mass of partners and competitors to realize a higher standard of practice:

- **Public pressure.** Media and public exposure of the kind provided by Greenpeace pressures key buyers and is an essential catalyst for action.

- **Trust among parties.** Cannon cites "calm and measured dialogue between the buyers, NGO pressure groups, and experts" as critical to keeping all parties at the table. Langert found that constructive dialogue requires a credible broker—an entity like Cannon's organization—with impeccable credentials and the support of hard facts and science, to build trust.

- **Private self-interest.** Finally, and importantly, is the need for a collective and intelligent response from the supply chain of private actors, who ultimately benefit over the long term from attacking the problem at *the source*.

Underlying these ingredients is the need for a diversity of perspectives at the table, to ensure that the solutions address aspects of the problem that may not be apparent to the market-based principals—and that offer both out-of-the-box thinking and accountability. The table must accommodate those who speak for the health of the commons.

To eliminate overfishing in the Barents Sea also required reaching a critical mass of buyers and sellers. The entire fishery was at risk. Espersen brought other producers with significant market exposure to the table. Peers with reputations at stake and customer relationships to protect enabled a new industry standard to emerge. By working together, the trade group devised a solution that offered bad operators no place to turn.

THE ARCHITECTS OF CHANGE: MARKET-BASED COALITIONS AND CIVIL SOCIETY ORGANIZATIONS

In his book *Responsible Leadership: Lessons from the Front Line of Sustainability and Ethics*, Sir Mark Moody-Stuart describes his experience with coalitions like the one in the Barents Sea. I enjoyed many conversations with Mark, from the first Aspen dialogue he attended in 1999 on the role of corporations while serving as CEO of Royal Dutch Shell Group, and on through his chairmanship of Anglo American in the mid-2000s.

One of Mark's great strengths was a genuine curiosity about the people he would meet at all levels of society across Shell's massive footprint. He has a keen appreciation for human nature, and the values that he and his intrepid wife, Judy, embraced and that guided decisions through 10 posts at country offices of Shell made him a highly sought-after adviser to many organizations, including the United Nations.

I remember sitting on the south bank of the River Thames, in front of Shell's London headquarters, cramming for a meeting with Mark early on in my tenure at the Aspen Institute. I hoped to persuade him to co-chair our business dialogue the following summer in Aspen. Sitting on the grass, I read through the first ever *People, Planet, Profits* report on the company's social impact and responsibilities. Shell was among the first global companies to issue a CSR report; it was known in the biz as the *Tell Shell* report because it utilized frank feedback and criticism from adversaries and agitators to learn from, speak to, and help set the agenda for the work ahead.

I was totally disarmed by the fresh language and transparent reporting on how the company measured up against its principles on the environment, labor, human rights, and corruption. The report included a postcard to send in comments. Reading the report gave a window into Mark's open style of leadership. He was a great listener, and whenever he opened his mouth, what he had to say was worth hearing. I learned a lot from him about the chain of actors between consumer and brand on the one hand, and natural resources and labor markets on the other. "You know," he once said to me casually while we were in line at the salad bar, "the brand isn't really your problem; the ones you need to worry about are the ones with *no brand* to protect."

Mark dedicates a chapter of his book to these market-based coalitions and alliances with civil society organizations that employ dialogue and shared commitment to build trust with critics and among competitors, and to deepen understanding about how private self-interest connects to higher operating standards.

CO-CREATION AMONG COMPETITORS WHEN THE LICENSE TO OPERATE IS AT RISK

One of Mark's many engagements has been with the International Council on Mining and Metals (ICMM), created by nine of the largest mining entities to respond to the "resource curse"—the prevalence of poverty, poor labor conditions, and environmental decline in regions with abundant mineral resources but weak rule of law.

ICMM's commitment to research, transparency, and continuous improvement was set out by the founders in 2002. Dialogue among peers led to a set of principles designed to hold themselves, and eventually their industry, accountable to international standards on labor, human rights, and the environment. A report 10 years out found both real progress and new challenges to contend with, but the organization had also grown in scope and today represents 27 significant mining companies, each of which is vetted against the standards of the collective, plus 36 industry and commodities associations and affiliates across the world.

One of the themes that emerge in Mark's remarkable book—described as part autobiography, part confessional—is about the importance of the local business networks baked into regional associations and communities.

When Kofi Annan, as UN secretary-general, launched the UN Global Compact in 1999, he welcomed 40 international companies to the table, Shell and Unilever among them. Each member committed to report against a set of nine principles based on UN conventions on human rights, labor, and the environment and a tenth principle to address corruption and pressure to pay bribes.

Today there are more than 12,000 signatories from 160 countries. The UNGC members and affiliates commit to the principles designed to raise the bar on complex business-society issues and have access to opportunities for peer learning among leaders of industry.

Mark knows from decades of experience in oil and gas and mining that the endgame is about both transparency and accountability on the ground; it is in the host communities where the impact of business decisions, for good or for ill, is felt most directly. The real dynamism within the UN Global Compact resides in the local networks, where business managers and executives throughout the world can meet across the breakfast table to consider the priorities that are most important in their own region, such as human rights in China or issues involving migrant labor in Bangladesh and Dubai.

The emphasis on local networks recalls the Committee for Economic Development's challenge of job creation after World War II. It's in community that the nature of relationships and the codependencies and personal ties between business and other vital institutions are abundantly clear.

Mark's other key message about collaborative efforts is that they are most effective when the objective is "clear but limited."

The Better Cotton Initiative (BCI) is one of the fastest growing of the business-society networks. It illustrates the need for both localization and specialization.

BCI was started as a project of WWF's initiative on commodities. Its approach, in important respects, is the polar opposite of the targeted campaign to eliminate overfishing in the Barents Sea region. Cotton is a commodity with many uses that in one way or another contributes to the livelihood of an estimated 250 million people around the world. The United States is a major producer, along with Uzbekistan, China, and India, but cotton is grown in warm climates on every continent.

As BCI's website makes clear, there are no guarantees for their members about physical traceability of the product.

Members of the organization include fashion lines, along with producers at every stop along the supply chain: from growing and harvesting to multistep processes for turning cotton into yarn and then into fabric for clothing or myriad industrial uses. Clothing manufacturers and retailers who source their materials globally may be under pressure to eliminate the use of pesticides or inhumane labor practices in the supply chain, but they are unable to make definitive claims about their product.

The Marine Stewardship Council's ratings of fish varieties and the Forest Stewardship Council's certification of sustainably harvested wood products rely on traceability of the products. When it comes to cotton, a step change in the labor and environmental practices requires an entirely different model of co-creation. You have to tackle the entire market.

The Better Cotton strategy links manufacturers and retailers all the way back to the farmers. To see real change across markets requires steady increases in the number of producers committed to practices of fair labor, environmental sustainability, and resource conservation. There is no other way to approach the problem when the chain of custody is so complex.

The number of producers at the BCI table is impressive; in 2019, cotton certified against the Better Cotton standards represented 19 percent of the global market and is on track to achieve much higher penetration. The issues are remarkably complex: protections against child labor, pesticide use and runoff, equitable wages and worker safety, the effects of climate change and management for drought and extreme weather. The organization has provided training on sustainable agriculture practices to more than 2.2 million farmers in 21 countries.

Technology is also playing a role; experiments with blockchain are deployed in an attempt to tag and trace the origins of cotton supplies. Two inventive members of our forum for chief sustainability officers, Michael Kobori of Levi Strauss and Mark Mason of the commodity trader Cargill, collaborated on a project to influence commodity trading and to separate out organic cotton as a discrete tradable product.

But the consumer, for the most part, just wants a good-looking pair of jeans at an affordable price—and maybe a hint of security that the product is clean of noxious practices. The interests of the retailers and manufacturers with a brand to protect offer the glue and impetus for the steady growth in membership in BCI. They motivate unbranded, B2B producers to come to the table, where they are joined by a host of civil society actors representing discrete concerns in specific regions, from the economic security of laborers in Pakistan to exposure to chemicals for workers in China, to water scarcity and pollution in India.

It is hard to take in the scale of the Better Cotton Initiative. In Bryant Park terms, it's as if you are not allowed to completely enjoy your lunch in one beautiful urban space until all parks, everywhere, are safe and clean.

THE WORK AHEAD: LEADERSHIP FOR CO-CREATION

The story of the Barents Sea continues to unfold. Jim Cannon expects the region to be in the news again: "As the arctic ice recedes ever further . . . due to climate change, fishing boats are venturing ever further north and trawling on pristine habitat, including cold water coral areas."[8]

The problems that Cannon tackles in his organization are messy, complex, dynamic—seemingly intractable. Cannon has the vision, emotional intelligence, and commitment required to identify the first movers, help them envision a different future, and unlock the change needed in partnership with others.

Critics find the voluntary initiatives that link producers and consumers lacking; they want the clarity of law and regulation and visible punishment of scofflaws. Progress comes in fits and starts as campaigners and the consumer face reluctant leaders and investors. But in a global world, there are no command-and-control answers.

Even the most tangible change in business requires a special kind of leader—one who can subordinate his or her ego and link his or her ambition and skills to something larger, to root cause analysis and systemic change. Mark Moody Stuart of Shell, Bob Langert of McDonald's, and Klaus Nielsen of Espersen are able to listen to critics but also work with their suppliers and even their competitors.

TACKLING CLIMATE CHANGE

The ultimate systems challenge for business leaders, and the rest of us, of course, is climate change. We need pricing policy to catch up with a shift in mindset and make the markets work—both to increase the cost of the status quo energy sources and to ramp up investment in carbon capture and in new sources of energy, including next-generation nuclear power.[9] The consequences of ignoring the problem, or depending on voluntary initiatives only, are just too great. The need for business leadership on policy change in the United States is acute.

As the COVID-19 pandemic was emerging in the winter of 2019, the Business Roundtable was preparing to release a policy statement and recommendations on addressing climate change. The process of study and dialogue among members and experts was thorough, and the result carefully guarded, but as the date for going public came closer, I heard from colleagues that the statement was strong and compelling. I became more confident that with the BRT's shoulder to the wheel, we could, at last, begin to break the logjam on forging federal policy.

Broad-based business trade associations like the BRT stay alive by avoiding controversy among members and by focusing on win-win policies for which there is broad agreement in business—like public investment in education and workforce training and lowering corporate taxes. When it comes to a massively complex system like energy policy, it's infinitely more complex to agree on a policy solution. Greenhouse gases are the product of industrialization and consumer demand for power, and the massive changes required to avoid catastrophic impacts of global warming touch every part of industry and commerce. There are winners and losers—both belong to the BRT.

Under the US system of private influence of public policy, it is impossible to move the needle if our most influential business network stays on the sidelines or leaves the microphone in the hands of the naysayers. The BRT protocols for taking policy positions don't typically embrace the kind of diversity of voices and interests that we see in the coalitions described in this chapter.

However, after years of nudging from environmental campaigners, and from other business networks and conveners like my own organization, and with careful stewardship by staff within the BRT and its member companies, the long view had finally won out. The costs of inaction were too high. And these leaders, many of them, were already on record about the need for policy change. The rest were hearing from their own employees and family members.

I heard from colleagues in BRT companies that an overwhelming number of the CEOs had signed off on the last draft of the policy paper. Based on the attention the organization received for its statement on the purpose of the corporation in the summer of 2019, I expected a surge of interest—and the potential, at last, for business-supported public policy to catch up with overwhelming public opinion on the need for change.

At this writing, the proposed BRT climate policy is stalled. As we moved rapidly into "social distancing" and shutdown due to the COVID-19 surge in March 2020 and all travel and events were canceled, the launch event was postponed indefinitely, and it was deemed impossible in this moment to create the space for substantive discussion of climate—or much of anything else.

But in a funny way, the climate crisis has both receded from view and moved to center stage. At this writing, the air is clean in Los Angeles and Shanghai for the first time in decades. Biking is now the best way to get around New York.

Can it last? Does this moment of crisis offer a real opportunity, or will we fail to capture the moment? What if this is the opportunity we have been waiting for?

The shock to the system from the coronavirus, on top of years of deteriorating trade conditions, could force a reevaluation of the "take, make, dispose" model and allow, at last, a shift to the decades-in-the-making business design principles of a circular economy. Businesses built on extensive global supply chains have to consider a Plan B.

Teams inside our most capacious companies are impatiently waiting for the chance to design products and business models that work for the planet.

The Business Roundtable's acknowledgment of the multiple stakeholders who exist alongside shareholders opens the door for new ideas to emerge. Will supportive protocols (and regulations) that are needed for systemic change follow? Will coalitions of businesses and labor convene to rethink the share of wealth that goes into the pockets of workers? Will share buybacks again be regulated as stock manipulation, and will tax avoidance schemes that undermine local infrastructure and services finally become intolerable? Will companies consider those who are most vulnerable in the global economy and redirect their government relations teams to prioritize the health of the commons?

Investment—both public and private—to fix a crumbling health care system and build the green infrastructure of the future must rise to the top of the priority list. Shareholders will benefit too, over time.

Real change in business priorities will always face headwinds, but that's where leadership comes in. And we all have a role to play, as investors, consumers, and citizens. As the journalist and social activist Dorothy Day was known to say, "No one has a right to sit down and feel hopeless. There is too much work to do."

Sometimes, the most effective change agents are found inside the business.

Within every corporation, capable, courageous staff and managers with a belief in business as a powerful platform for change are stepping up on complex problems. To be effective, they need to tell a good story and paint a vision of what is possible. These skills are found in our colleagues who manage CSR and sustainability efforts across global enterprises. They also exist in the front lines of purchasing departments and supply chain management, and even in staff functions like human resources—and the CFO's office. For these exceptional leaders, co-creation is the norm, not the exception.

The stories collected from the Aspen First Movers Fellowship are drawn from years of supporting change agents in every industry and across every corporate function. The fellows improve the protocols for use of private data, incubate new approaches for reducing carbon emissions, and create revenue-generating businesses that utilize waste or help people without bank accounts access financial services.

The two-decade-plus turnaround of Bryant Park is a miniature blueprint for the work ahead of us now: the importance of small wins and the need for more leaders able to innovate at the intersection of private enterprise and public benefit.

Perhaps the greatest inhibitor of influencing capitalism as we experience it now is the failure to imagine anything different. Reading the stories of Jim Cannon and Jason Clay and their counterparts working inside businesses remind us that deep change is possible.

Business executives don't get out of bed in the morning and wring their hands in despair—they are wired to find the opportunity in crisis, even in the throes of a pandemic. The same is true of visionary leaders in other domains. It's about the complex interplay of commerce and culture. When public interest and business needs are aligned, extraordinary change is possible.

CHAPTER SEVEN

The Road Ahead: The Design of Incentives to Unlock Real Value

It is difficult to get a man to understand something, when his salary depends on his not understanding it.

—SINCLAIR LEWIS

DONELLA MEADOWS wrote the book on systems thinking, literally. In *Thinking in Systems: A Primer*, she says that a system is "a set of things—people, cells, molecules, or whatever—interconnected in such a way that they produce their own pattern of behavior over time."[1] She lays out the leverage points for systems change, from least important to most important. The key takeaway from her work is that the greatest leverage exists in the *design* of the system, the setting of intentions—influencing the *mindset.**

---

* Meadows is well known for her early work with colleagues, *The Limits to Growth: A Report for the Club of Rome's Project on the Predicament of Mankind*, which opened a debate in 1972 that continues today about the capacity of the Earth to support population growth and economic expansion.

In business, the ways we educate, orient, and reward executives are a signal of what matters most. Education and dialogue can be a pathway to unlocking intentions and behavior. To ensure that intention has room to grow—to give it gravitas, to enable it to gain influence and reach a tipping point—requires what is measured and rewarded to be aligned.

CEO pay is much discussed and analyzed in the United States because of stratospheric levels of compensation in a number of publicly traded companies and hedge funds. However, a more important reason to focus on pay is the role it plays in *system design*. What are we paying executives to *do*? When chief executives say they are committed to their "stakeholders," do the financial rewards align with their goals?

The massive shift toward equity-based pay that began in the 1980s has produced runaway CEO pay and a premium for stockholders at the expense of employees and long-term investment. Placing the stock price at the center of compensation undermines the new rules and the call to CEOs to lead on issues of consequence for the benefit of both the business and society.

The CEO matters; how she thinks, or what he values, is a critically important starting point for change. We need to redesign pay to catch up with the intentions of executives to serve society.

But before we wade into the murky and complex domain of executive compensation, it may be useful to take a closer look at the CEO's mindset. It's not a logic model or business case that influences how a CEO thinks or convinces him or her to take a bold step; it's often something that cuts deeper to the bone. We can't engineer that kind of experience, although sophisticated NGOs are pretty good at it, but we can ensure that the signals they receive from boards and long-term investors reinforce the behaviors and decisions we hope for.

In the late summer of 2019, the CEO members of the Business Roundtable signed on to a statement that spoke powerfully to the complexity of managing their companies. The needs of a range of constituents were paramount; they rejected the idea that public companies must prioritize the shareholders. A chorus of voices responded—many enthusiastic, some cynical, others critical. The Council of Institutional Investors called out the statement for what it was, a chipping away at the primacy of shareholder interests.

The forces that led to the statement and give power to the new rules that are influencing decision-making are irreversible: the growing importance of intangible sources of value; radical transparency and the power of social media and employee voice; and the relative decline in importance of financial capital. The urgency of climate change and species decline, and abiding concern for inequality and injustice, are a rallying cry for co-creating generative processes and valuing workers and community.

These forces must prevail; will business respond before it is forced to do so through even more explosive social movements or the ballot box?

"The American dream is alive but fraying," Jamie Dimon, CEO of JPMorgan Chase, said when he issued the statement in his role as chairman of the BRT. "These modernized principles reflect the business community's unwavering commitment to continue to push for an economy that serves all Americans." Alex Gorsky, CEO of Johnson & Johnson, said the statement "better reflects the way corporations can and should operate."

With all their power and influence and command of resources, what do these CEOs aim to do now? How will they employ their license to operate—and know if they are on track? Where do they get their cues?

We are in a race against time.

THE PROBLEM WITH FACTS

Among those who penned a response to the BRT's call to action was Marc Benioff, CEO of Salesforce and an outspoken critic of shareholder primacy. In an opinion piece published in the *New York Times*, he counseled business leaders to look at the facts: "Research shows that companies that embrace a broader mission—and, importantly, integrate that purpose into their corporate culture—outperform their peers, grow faster, and deliver higher profits."[2]

Benioff's intentions are good, but there's a problem with his advice: facts rarely, if ever, influence the actions or priorities of a leader wired for a different reality. Data may help break through what one of our fellows called the "mud layer of middle management," but it rarely resets the intentions of key decision makers.

In fact, after decades of experimentation, perhaps we should question whether ubiquitous metrics-based ratings and rankings of companies across industries are actually doing anything useful when it comes to changing behavior below the surface.

The architecture of systemic change is built through direct and meaningful experience, not metrics. Take, for example, the decision of CVS to stop selling cigarettes. It emerged from a fresh look at the fundamental purpose of the enterprise. Did their stores enable health and well-being, or not? Delta's progressive profit-sharing plan was born of deep crisis and the prospect of total failure; in order to emerge from bankruptcy able to build a better future, the company needed to enlist everyone involved—and find a way to motivate pilots and everyone else who had to absorb significant pay cuts.

We can look to a meaningful number of customer service enterprises, including Panera Bread, Costco, Market Basket, QuikTrip, the Container Store, Starbucks, and Southwest, who have broken with convention to offer higher pay and benefits and who respect workers as the heart of the business plan. Data and examples reinforced the business model; they were not the impetus.

Chip and Dan Heath, in their best-selling book *Switch: How to Change Things When Change Is Hard*, describe this phenomenon as the difference between the actions of the elephant and its rider.[†] The rider is operating from reason; he has the knowledge and the plan.

---

† Jonathan Haidt was first to use the metaphor of the rider and the elephant in his book *The Happiness Hypothesis* (2006).

The elephant is all instinct and emotion. It might be hungry, tired, or fearful. It stops along the way or may suddenly change direction or refuse to stop. Moving along the path of change requires both the rider's plan and the momentum of the elephant. Getting *started* on the path, however, is more about the instincts of the elephant brain than the reasoning of the rider brain.

The wake-up call to the CEO comes with a swift kick in the rear from an aggressive campaign, or an encounter with an employee in the cafeteria or parking lot, or a provocative question at the all-hands or from his kid at the kitchen table. These personal experiences take executives to the heart of the matter; they enable change in how he or she perceives and calculates value—they have the power to change what one *believes*.

INFLUENCING THE MINDSET OF LEADERS

Lee Scott was CEO of Walmart in the 2000s. With roughly 1.5 million part-time and full-time workers in the United States, Walmart was then, and is today the largest private employer, running neck and neck with the federal government. The company has close to 5,000 stores across the country and more than 11,000 worldwide. Its supply chain is vast, its global footprint unmeasurable.

During Scott's tenure, Walmart was buffeted by a campaign that coordinated pressure from labor unions and environmental NGOs. The well-supported operation was designed to draw the public's attention to the social and environmental consequences of a business model that adheres to "Always Lowest Price." It challenged whether the company was giving as much as it was getting from host communities, suppliers, and workers. It began years earlier, but within a short time of Lee Scott's becoming the CEO in 2000, the ground campaign had enough success in some regions of North America and Europe to make it almost impossible for Walmart to plan for new distribution centers in service of new stores in Germany and in parts of Canada, New England, and California.

Then, in 2005, Hurricane Katrina hit the Gulf of Mexico and went on to wreak havoc on New Orleans and along the Gulf coastline. Lee Scott and Walmart kicked into action, responding to the emergency with the same operational efficiency that kept shelves stocked across the country.

Overnight, Walmart sent a score of tractor trailers loaded with blankets, water, food, and diapers to the epicenter of the storm, while local store managers gave away stranded inventory to help neighbors in need. A photo of Walmart trucks made it onto the front page of virtually every newspaper in the country; they were lined up as far as the eye could see along Interstate 10, waiting for the National Guard to reopen the roads into the heart of New Orleans. This singular image offered the best press the company had seen in a decade.

During a listening tour to understand the company's critics and engage its managers and employees. Scott posed this question: "What would it take for Walmart to be that company, at our best, all the time?"

The answer, gleaned from feedback across hundreds of encounters, came in a remarkable speech by Scott to his employees in October 2005—a little more than a month after the storm abated. Released publicly under the title "Twenty First Century Leadership," it set extensive and aggressive goals that Walmart would pursue to move well beyond the charitable acts that were so visible in the wake of Katrina, to engage the business itself in leading change.

Scott called the conduct of business as usual a "Katrina in slow motion" and pledged to enlist the company's massive supply chain in operational changes and new standards for procurement that the company believed would drop straight to the bottom line—from greater fuel efficiency and dematerializing packaging to increasing sustainably harvested products in the product mix and preferences for suppliers able to match Walmart's goals on the reduction of greenhouse gases.

Scott also spoke to the human face of their operations. Relative to the precise signals on the environmental front, Scott's 2005 message on investment in low-wage earners in stores and distribution centers feels tepid. Some important changes have taken place since that moment, and while Walmart continues to be criticized for moving slowly on worker pay, Scott did open the door with a call for a higher federal minimum wage—a goal that the current CEO, Doug McMillon, has the opportunity to directly influence as the new chairman of the Business Roundtable.

The Lee Scott moment was a game-changer. Walmart invited product sellers to come to Bentonville, Arkansas, to meet with the buyers and to start the process of building alliances with key suppliers, including many that are massive companies in their own right.

The Walmart story is not a fairy tale. Some of the changes have been easy but many have not. The story is still unfolding. In 2015, the company's chief sustainability officer, Kathleen McLaughlin, reflected on its progress against the aspirations of a decade earlier, stating, "We have celebrated some important milestones and accomplishments and have also struggled with obstacles and failures. We have learned a lot about what works and what doesn't when it comes to achieving lasting change."[3]

When your business model is built to deliver on low price and convenience, it's complicated to lead on higher product and labor standards. Walmart is the single largest seller of many products we depend on, and like its chief competitor, Amazon, it enables the consumer's magical thinking about low prices without consequences. But Lee Scott's epiphany and the journey that began with Walmart's suppliers in the wake of Hurricane Katrina was a shot across the bow for the business community. Scott's leadership of Walmart in 2005 was evidence of a fundamental shift in mindset; it started new conversations in more boardrooms than we probably give him credit for.

Metrics mostly document what we already believe to be true. Facts can support the changes—but they rarely cause the change.

In his provocative book *Winners Take All: The Elite Charade of Changing the World*, Anand Giridharadas, an Aspen Institute Henry Crown Fellow, tackles inequality and the rules of the system that enable the winners to continue to gain ground at the expense of the middle class. He challenges what he calls *Market World*—"the concurrent drives to do well and do good, to change the world while also profiting from the status quo."[4]

Giridharadas criticizes those who call for concrete solutions to big social problems but fail to challenge enablers such as preferential taxes on capital over labor and shareholder-centric measures that reward the outsourcing of jobs or keep wages low. Giridharadas questions the net value of philanthropy and so-called social enterprise. He posits that it's not enough to do something good—i.e., you can't ignore the negative consequences of a business decision by being generous with some of the profits.

Giridharadas raises pointed questions about those of us who elevate business as positive agents of change and points back to the underlying questions of what a business, at its core, is designed to do.

Business is not by any means the whole answer, but we can't ignore it either. I am remembering the words of Nitin Nohria in the preface to this book: "None of the major problems confronting the globe today—sustainability, health care, poverty, financial-system repair—can be solved unless business plays a significant role."[5]

CAN BUSINESS LEAD?

If we can't depend on every executive having a road-to-Damascus experience like that of Lee Scott or Phil Knight of Nike a generation earlier, what is needed now to achieve a real shift in the mindset of leaders? And what keeps the old rules in place?

Many members of the Business Roundtable concluded that it was right—even easy—to sign on to a statement that supplanted "shareholder primacy" with "stakeholder management" because they believed they were already doing what was required.

Businesses that grow to the scale of the membership of the BRT *do* care about their employees, support their host community, and scrub the supply chain for noxious labor and environmental practices. And yet, inequality grows and the planet is warming. The real story is told in the growth in share buybacks, in contracts with advisory services to maximize tax avoidance, and especially in how we compensate executives.

WHAT ARE WE PAYING EXECUTIVES TO DO?

In 2018, companies began to publish new data about pay—fulfilling a mandate laid down by Congress in the wake of the 2008 financial meltdown. Each year, publicly listed corporations analyze and release a comparison between the CEO's pay package and a measure of the median pay for the rest of the employees.

The new data offers a complicated yet, ultimately, revealing picture of the culture and values of public companies. This comparison of the CEO's pay with the median, along with the requirement that the company periodically poll shareholders about the pay for the chief executive, is designed to elevate the CEO's pay as a matter of debate.

But the results from these so-called Say on Pay votes suggest that investors don't care if the CEO makes 100 or even 1,000 times the income of the median worker, as long as the stock price is rising. Laborers are also mostly silent on executive pay; they care much more about their own share of the pie than if the CEO is compensated at a level that is almost impossible for most Americans to take in. And trends suggest that greater transparency about what other CEOs make has an unintended consequence: even higher pay thresholds.

In one case I recently learned about, the CEO's pay had increased fivefold in the 20 years since the company went public, while the average factory worker's pay declined by a fifth. Is this CEO overpaid? Not in conventional competitive terms, or even through the lens of cost-benefit analysis—that is, if the measure of benefit is the stock price. This executive's pay would never make a list of the highest-paid CEOs. Even if it did, the pay at the top barely matters when it comes to overall profits. There is only one CEO in a company—except in the most outrageous examples, it's a minor cost factor in the overall scheme of things.

The United States is a global outlier when it comes to pay levels for the CEO and executive team. At the top end of the scale, earning a CEO salary is like hitting the lottery year after year after year, with the pot growing most years, while worker pay on average is flat; this is a source of political discontent, decline in trust in business, and greater inequality than we have experienced since the 1920s. The people who make the product, handle customers, and do the unseen jobs that support these efforts haven't seen a raise in decades, even as rates of productivity increased.

A recent theme in the growing conversation about what to do about CEO pay says that you don't fix inequality by attacking CEOs— you need to address the problem bottom-up. (Surely both are needed.) But reducing "quantum," as the market jocks call the CEO's earnings, is only one part of a bigger problem rarely discussed by directors who defend the CEO's pay as a function of competition.

But there is a bigger issue at stake.

Even more important than the *amount* of pay is the *design* of pay— the intentions that underlie the structure of rewards and incentives. Incentives, of course, should align with the goals and expectations of management, but in spite of all the discussion of stakeholders, the pay-for-performance system that dominates boardrooms and class-rooms is still heavily weighted toward shareholders—i.e., share price. Executives are given stock grants or stock-based incentives to assure that the management team stays focused on share value—or is justly rewarded for higher stock valuations, depending on your point of view.

There are at least two reasons for the stickiness of shareholder value as the dominant signal in pay. One is *agency theory*, a seductive but flawed idea designed to keep managers beholden to their shareholders. Ensuring that the managers of your enterprise are truly your "agents," working on your behalf, made sense when a group of investors were financing a railroad or building a factory and bore all of the risk.

But the stock market no longer works that way. Professional man-agers of global enterprises are not working for the shareholders in any practical sense of the word. The board, which hires the executive, has a fiduciary duty first and foremost to the long-term health of the enterprise, not the holders of shares of stock. Weighing down executives with equity-based incentives keeps the system tethered to shareholders. To reward executives principally in stock is problematic for the reasons detailed in this book and by a chorus of critics in business and beyond. In addition, there is a practical problem: which shareholder are we talking about? Shareholders as a class actually don't have much in common—their interests and time horizons are very broad.

The second reason executives are paid in stock is that in spite of a growing conversation about the need to be attuned to all of the inputs for long-term success, the share price is still the master of the realm in public company boards. Proxy advisory firms like Institutional Shareholder Services (ISS) and Glass Lewis issue recommendations to asset managers and mutual funds. Most follow their advice, which hews to whatever is needed to enhance the value of the shares. One of the classic ways to do that is to ensure that the stock price is the loudest signal in the pay package. The protocols of boards and their advisers who benchmark pay against other public companies reinforce the status quo.

How does pay for performance work in reality?

Equilar is a private advisory firm that benchmarks CEO pay. From its 2018 public release, we know that the CEO of a typical large public company now receives only about 10 percent of his or her compensation in cash, and the balance in stock and equity-linked incentives. In addition to high CEO pay, the focus on shareholder value and the massive shift toward equity-based pay that began in the mid-1980s go hand-in-hand with growth in share repurchases resulting in a premium to stockholders—who take the share of the pie that used to go to the employees. The principal beneficiaries include the executives themselves.

The system of incentives and rewards is perfectly aligned to produce what we see in play today: high returns to shareholders and low investment in productive uses of profits to spur innovation and public goods—i.e., investment in workforce development, wages, R&D, and quality assurance on the shop floor and through the supply chain.

The historic link between wage growth and productivity growth is now broken. In low-wage industries like retail, the contrast between share repurchases and wages is illustrative of systemic failure.

In the restaurant industry, for example, researchers from the Roosevelt Institute and the National Employment Law Project found that between 2015 and 2017, share repurchases (or share buybacks) measured *136 percent of profits.*[6] Their findings mine the connections between stock-centric executive compensation, tremendous growth in share buybacks, and sluggish economic growth and low pay—a national embarrassment during an era of massive wealth accumulation.

THE COST OF SHARE BUYBACKS

The largest share of the distribution to shareholders is accomplished through companies buying back their own shares to bump up the stock price, a practice that naturally enriches those with the most stock. Cases of companies borrowing to buy up more shares are commonplace—and explain how a company can distribute more profits in a given year than it actually earns. While it might make sense for a company to buy its own stock when management is convinced that the stock is undervalued for some reason, this rationale doesn't hold up under scrutiny.

Until the 1980s, the practice of share buybacks was prohibited as a form of market manipulation. Today, taking special measures to boost the stock price is the *point.*

The individual who has probably done more than anyone to bring our attention to the national plague of share buybacks is William Lazonick, a Harvard-trained economist who earned his PhD in 1975. Lazonick teaches economics at UMass Lowell, situated in the historic mill town whose concentration of textile factories in the 1800s earned it the name, "cradle of the American industrial revolution."

As a researcher, Lazonick was originally drawn to economic development and investment in innovation. He became interested in the relationship between the "productive economy" and the "financial economy" after shareholder value theory began to take management theory by storm, beginning at Harvard in the mid-1980s and spreading quickly from there to other scholars and institutions.

Lazonick ultimately created the Academic-Industry Research Network, to link like-minded scholars and industry experts. The Network researchers looked at the data between 2008 and 2017 and found that share buybacks had increased to the extent that 94 percent of profits were distributed to shareholders in the form of buybacks plus dividends over the course of the decade. In March 2019, Senator Tammy Baldwin reintroduced the Reward Work Act—to curb buybacks and give workers a greater say in decision-making at their companies—and asked Lazonick to appear at a Senate hearing as an expert witness for the bill.

Rick Wartzman of the Drucker Institute and Lazonick looked again at the numbers in the wake of the Trump tax cuts, which were sold to the public as a reinvestment in American productivity and the American worker. They determined that the trend was continuing.

The 2017 corporate tax cuts reduced the statutory rate from 36 percent to 24 percent. The actual rate paid by companies that year, on average, after the application of credits and various schemes to reduce tax exposure, was 9 percent. The long wait for a lower tax rate was over. It no longer made sense to shield the cash in offshore locations to avoid high tax rates at home. Companies were now awash in cash.

JUST Capital, which began polling Americans about their attitudes and expectations of corporations in 2015, began to track statements by companies in the Russell 1000 as the tax windfall began to hit. For the first 145 companies that announced their intentions, the benefit to workers amounted to 6 percent of the tax relief; most of it was in the form of onetime bonuses, not permanent pay raises. Companies were also expected to utilize tax savings to invest in job creation, but the pattern was already clear. Stock buybacks that rewarded wealth would swamp investment in work, again.

Current CEO pay levels for many public companies make those companies look like an airline, where the only person who matters is the pilot—not the ground crew or the flight attendants or reservation clerks, or the quality control tinkerers, and certainly not the men and women who work behind the scenes: who wrangle the ore and fuel from the ground, forge the parts, tighten the bolts, and solder the frame—or serve the food in the cafeteria or clean the restroom late into the night.

In tech and other industries, a growing segment of the workforce is now hidden, employed by contractors who make it easier to cut wages and benefits in the name of competitiveness.

Pay for performance directly undermines the spirit of the BRT's revolutionary statement on stakeholder value. When the company prioritizes the stock price, the productive capacity of the firm is undermined, and whether it happens at Apple, Citibank, General Electric, or Merck, we all lose—not just workers.

Boards seem complicit—or at least compliant. They take signals from investors, and in one sense they are doing what they are asked to do—and increasingly are *paid* to do. Directors, like the CEO—are often given stock grants or rewarded with incentives tied to the stock price.

And what is the result of decades of focus on the shareholders?

- Low employee engagement scores and productivity gains that no longer reward the employees who produce them

- Unions in decline, viewed as a drag on competitiveness and efficiency

- Low levels of investment in retraining despite the massive shift in job content due to technology and growth in artificial intelligence

- Decline in the US share of global business R&D

- ◆ Levels of inequality, according to World Bank data, that place the United States on par with Argentina and the Ivory Coast, and well above norms throughout Europe, including the Baltics, the UK, and Scandinavia

- ◆ Communities fractured by a lack of economic opportunity

◆ ◆ ◆

These consequences have opened a new conversation about how we pay executives. The conversation is about the connections between an employee of the company and a contractor with a similar job but with no benefits or job security. It is about the balance of financial and nonfinancial goals, from targets on reducing greenhouse gases to greater diversity. It is about transparency, about aligning pay with purpose, and about long-term focus. It is about fairness.

UNLEASHING CREATIVITY IN THE DESIGN OF PAY

An important strand of this conversation is taking place among scholars, executives, and professional advisers who believe that stock-based compensation impedes sound judgment and carries unintended consequences.

From the science of behavior and research into motivation we know that goals can be powerful incentives, but they don't work as intended for positions that require critical-thinking skills. Michael Dorff, corporate governance scholar and author of *Indispensable and Other Myths: Why the CEO Pay Experiment Failed and How to Fix It*, explains that incentives work best for rote assignments and piece-work, but not for jobs that rely on judgment and EQ.[7]

We also know that long-term rewards lose their power over time. The mantra about using stock to reward *long-term* behavior is also a myth. Incentives are most effective when they are felt immediately. So while good managers can influence the stock value over the long term, it's not because their incentives tie them to the grindstone. To the contrary; recent examples, from Valeant to VW, Wells Fargo to Boeing, illustrate how paying executives in stock drives short-term behavior to "make the number."

Finally, the notion of "felt fairness" is at risk when too great a disparity exists between layers: when the gap gets too big, teamwork, engagement, individual agency, and creativity begin to shred.

There are companies and executives who believe in the logic behind felt fairness and have experimented with new norms, even when their competitors reached pay ratios between the CEO and the average worker of 100 to 1, or even 250 to 1.

Intel was pursing greater productivity, employee agency, and teamwork when it set a goal in 2009 to keep the CEO's pay within a range of 1.5 to 3 times that of the EVPs. Peter Drucker strongly believed the CEO should make no more than 20 times the rank and file. Ben and Jerry's, when still led by its founders, committed to multiples so low as to be untenable. Paul Polman at Unilever hired a "global head of reward" and directed him to look at fairness from top to bottom.

In July 2020, the Bloomberg Pay Index released their CEO pay numbers for 2019. Robert Swan at Intel, at $99,022,847, made up mostly of stock grants and options, was ranked number seven.[8] It appears that felt fairness is no longer a priority.

But in other companies, the economic disruptions of COVID-19 are enabling a very different conversation.

To comply with changing norms amid the pandemic and in defiance of the conventions of proxy advisory firm ISS, Lloyds Bank in the UK announced in 2020 that they would pursue a new pay model for its top executives: switching incentive pay to long-term restricted shares. The CEO's maximum pay would actually decline, from 8.3 million pounds to 6.3 million ($7.7 million). ISS, however, still recommended a no vote on the plan, and over a third of the voting shareholders accepted the ISS recommendation and registered disapproval.

Why would ISS, which represents a range of institutional investors, recommend a vote against more reasonable pay?

The answer has to do with the old hobbyhorse of pay for performance—i.e., the degree of alignment with the stock value. The new pay scheme at Lloyds looks more like a long-term bonus plan than a true incentive plan, and ISS measures success in the most limited fashion: is the board paying the executives to put the stock value ahead of other considerations—even in a year in which branches are being closed and scores of employees laid off? Even when bailouts are required to keep the doors of many enterprises open?

How will the change take place?

◆ ◆ ◆

We need a different approach. And it requires more than tinkering with the pay-for-performance system that got us here. What if we looked at the health of the enterprise and its many parts rather than the chief executive?

When we shift the lens away from the CEO and instead focus on the company, new measures and metrics come into focus: employee engagement and retention, measures of productivity and customer service, and key risk factors buried in the supply chain.

Today, internal pay equity or fairness may still seem like an antique idea, but it is designed to build a strong and resilient culture. The reliance on measuring the CEO's pay against so-called peer groups of other CEOs helps to justify outsized pay packages but ignores the people who matter most—the CEO's own direct reports and managers—and then down the food chain to workers and employees who create the goods and services and engage with customers. To right-size the system, it works equally well to adjust from the bottom up.

Focusing on the employees who make up the enterprise may not resolve all of our questions about CEO pay, but it's a useful place to start—a thought experiment that can restore some common sense and creativity to a system that has become formulaic and stale.

Rethinking Pay for Performance: Five Questions for Directors

- **What are we paying the executive to do?** If the stock price or "total shareholder return" is the loudest signal in the pay package, what goals, values, and key constituents are we drowning out?

- **What do we need to be really good at for the company to flourish?** The corporate purpose and critical nonfinancial drivers of long-term value must be clear and have sufficient weight in any incentive plan along with financial measures. Clarify: what is a function of hiring well, and what truly merits a bonus or incentive.

- **What's the reason for the incentive pay?** Behavioral science is clear: incentives may work for piecework but have unintended consequences for jobs that require judgment and high EQ. (And incentives only really work in the short run.) A high-performing executive doesn't need an extra boost to build a strong culture or encourage innovation and long-term thinking. *Pay a good salary*—and reduce complex incentives and conditions.

- **Is the pay package designed with an eye to clear understanding?** If the executive is focused on a manageable number of high-priority goals, pay objectives can be summarized in a page or two and are readily understood by every director, along with investors, employees, *and* the CEO and his or her direct reports.

- **What's fair?** Focus on internal equity over external CEO-to-CEO benchmarks. Is the executive's pay fair relative to that of direct reports? How about between senior leaders and the employee population? And what's the right split of rewards between workers and shareholders?

MODERN PRINCIPLES OF SENSIBLE AND EFFECTIVE PAY

Executive pay has again become a lightning rod for criticism—a lens on business and the social contract.

Can the tsunami of change from COVID-19 and a surge in voluntary pay cuts by executives be the moment we have been waiting for?

Will it open the door to a fundamental rethinking of how we reward executives—of pay for performance? What would executive compensation look like if it were designed to build the internal organizational health of tomorrow's corporation—rather than benchmark and compare executives against one another?[‡]

It's hard to break the norms of the current system without buy-in from within—a core of leaders working together who share the commitment to change. We need to engage and cultivate a small group of directors and executives, or many groups—even dinner-party size to begin with—to discuss first principles and reset the norms in the wider system. We need case examples rooted in what we know to be true; executives may not be traded like baseball players, but they share their love of the game. The good ones focus on building a solid, long-term foundation for teamwork.

It will not be easy to identify directors who have the courage and conviction to move against conventions in the boardroom, but the need is clear. In their *Harvard Business Review* article "The Error at the Heart of Corporate Leadership," Joe Bower and Lynn Paine talk about how shareholder value theory "narrows management's field of vision" and how alignment of incentives with share price is, in fact, a moral hazard:

> When the interests of successive layers of management are "aligned" in this manner, the corporation may become so biased toward the narrow interests of its current shareholders that it fails to meet the requirements of its customers or other constituencies. In extreme cases it may tilt so far that it can no longer function effectively.[9]

Function effectively to what ends?

Tim Cook, of Apple Inc., leads one of the most influential companies on the planet. With a pay package of $133 million in 2019, he is

---

‡ In 2020, in partnership with Korn Ferry, the Aspen Institute Business and Society Program released a set of questions and principles under the title "Modern Principles of Sensible and Effective Pay" to help boards and executives consider new approaches to the design of rewards and incentives. One of the five principles is about fairness.

also one of the highest paid—a function of large stock grants ($122 million), plus a $7.7 million bonus, a $3 million salary, and $884,000 in perks. Cook ranked among the top 10 earners for two of the preceding three years as well.

In 2018, after the corporate tax cuts were enacted, Apple, then the largest company on the New York Stock Exchange, announced its intention to buy back $100 billion of stock, rewarding investors for their confidence in the company and its earning power, bolstering the stock price, and further concentrating wealth in the hands of those with the most stock. The price of Apple stock has quadrupled over the five years leading up to 2020. Stock repurchases topped $400 billion in that same period.

Cook readily admits that he doesn't need the money and said he would donate his massive earnings to charity. He would likely run the company the same way paid $10 million or $100 million. Could we imagine a different scenario for our most highly respected leaders of Silicon Valley?

Private enterprises like Apple have their pick of engineering talent and knowledge workers. In a world of hurt—a warming planet, disenfranchised workers, growing nativism, and disintegrating infrastructure—is there more we should expect from the company's license to operate?

What *could* Apple do with its gains? How might Apple and its peers pay it forward for the benefit of their own workforce and contractors, community, and country—and beyond? The tensions between private inurement and the public good are playing out in real time.

The examples of co-creation discussed in the last chapter offer compelling examples of what is possible when disparate voices that represent different parts of a broken system convene around a common goal. From rethinking electronic waste to retooling workers for the next decades, what is Apple uniquely equipped to do that will secure the long-term health of the business and the ecosystem on which the company is dependent?

Fixing pay and the incentive systems that undergird the system focused on share price is the next, critically important step along the path of real value creation. The best companies and executives will not fixate on unwinding the old system; they will build something new.

CHAPTER EIGHT

Ideas Worth Teaching

There is no finish line.

—T-SHIRT OF A JOGGER IN CENTRAL PARK

WHEN I LEFT the Ford Foundation in 1998 with a three-year grant to launch an initiative at the Aspen Institute, my focus was on what was taught in business schools. I hoped to stimulate dialogue in academic circles about how the purpose of business is framed in classrooms and sought to broaden the metrics of business success.

We have made progress; there is more to do. Business schools are part of a distinctive system with lots of critics but also a fair number of levers for change. To try to measure the value of business education is a lot like trying to define quality or "good art"; what is needed or found desirable evolves with the times, and with context. There is no end state. In this moment, the winds are shifting again.

For several decades, business has been the degree of choice for most senior executives with graduate degrees—supplanting degrees in engineering and law. The cost of higher education in an uncertain market may change the attraction of the two-year residential MBA, but the question remains: What is the impact of business schools on the mindset and intentions of business graduates, and what do we want the next generation of business students to learn?

Over the course of two decades and more, my colleagues and I have observed many great educators. One of the very best is Sally Blount. Sally finished a decade as dean at the Kellogg School of Management in 2019 and followed her heart to become CEO of Catholic Charities of Chicago, a job that requires every ounce of her knowledge of and experience with strategy and human behavior. When I first met Sally, she was the undergrad dean at NYU's Stern School of Business. She inspired us to create the Aspen Undergraduate Network to create peer learning opportunities for educators who integrate the liberal arts and humanities into college business teaching.

At a presentation before the trustees of the Aspen Institute while still leading Kellogg, Sally said that business is, by far, the most popular major on college campuses and has been for as long as data is available. Roughly 20 percent of US undergrads—350,000 students a year—enroll in business, not counting business minors and other certificate programs at colleges that don't offer a business major. MBA programs capture a quarter of our postgrads.

Therefore, Sally asserted, we need to make business education as "robust and broad as possible."

It's hard to overstate the weight and influence of business schools. So many people in the United States, and now globally, pursue degrees in business that it has spawned an entire industry of ratings and critique. Some of the criticism is damning. A recent book about Harvard Business School, the gold standard for graduate business education, was reviewed by James Stewart in the *New York Times Book Review*. Stewart summed up the perspective of the author, Duff McDonald, this way: the school's success and extraordinary reach make it positively "dangerous."[1]

Harvard, like its peers, teaches a shareholder-centric model of the firm, but Harvard is a big tent, and it is also a critically important platform for scholars and teachers who are keen to explore business models and metrics that align companies—and their managers—with the health of the planet.

HBS receives 10,000 applications in a typical year and accepts only a small fraction of them. It merits both criticism and accolades. And it has a monster endowment, was an early investor in online learning, and is not likely to slow down anytime soon.

While elite business schools that prepare their students for jobs on Wall Street and in professional service firms share the blame for promoting a simplistic and narrow measure of business success, mere criticism doesn't help scholars *move*. And we have no time to waste.

WINDS OF CHANGE IN BUSINESS EDUCATION

Rather than just admiring the problems created by "agency theory" and the shareholder-centric norms and practices, a league of pioneering faculty members are exploring the consequences of teaching to a single objective function. They appreciate that more is expected of business by employees, by next-generation managers, and by the public, but as management scholars, they are motivated by being able to better understand what makes firms perform well.

Joe Bower and Lynn Paine's article "The Error at the Heart of Corporate Leadership" is critically important because the authors utilize their knowledge of business decision-making and research craft to move public and private discourse rather than accept the status quo. They offer a window into a growing network of scholars working to provide a better road map for business decisions. They credit, and then build on, the work of dozens of academics who are steeped in corporate governance, corporate law, and business performance, and who, by asking useful questions, influence the questions in boardrooms and executive suites.

They also illustrate how academia works: how influential ideas take hold and shape scholarship for the generations to come. They acknowledge the work of generations of teachers who unpacked stakeholder theory for their students when the most intellectually curious among them were found only in ethics classrooms or electives on social impact or sustainability.

Today, in some disciplines, scholars are able to teach about decision models and frameworks that are useful to business managers migrating to generative business thinking and that blow the simplistic, single-objective function of shareholder value out of the water.

Jerry Davis at the Ross School of Management at the University of Michigan and Anne Tsui at the University of Notre Dame connect scholars in an organization called Responsible Research for Business and Management. Jerry and Anne and other scholars like Andy Hoffman, also at the University of Michigan, question the relevance of academic journal research; they aim to reassert the role of public scholars working on issues of consequence. And just in time. We need our best minds focused on issues that are on the critical path to a healthier society. Their energy and research insight bleed into the classroom. This is the kind of fresh thinking we need now, which helps build a new foundation for the "robust and broad" education that Sally Blount called for.

At my own alma mater, the Yale School of Management, and many business schools supported by the reach and capacity of a great university, this conversation has gone completely global and very 21st century. Yale has embraced virtual "networked learning" as a competitive advantage through the creation of the Global Network for Advanced Management (GNAM), which links faculty and students across the 29 member schools in real time, in such locations as Manila, Oxford, Singapore, Mexico, South Africa, Japan, Costa Rica, India, Israel, and Nigeria.

The curriculum features live, digitally enabled reports from MBA teams across the network. In a class called "The End of Globalization," students are challenged to think through the consequences of rising economic nationalism, anti-globalism, and populism, both in their own region and across every continent.

The Haas School of Business at the University of California, Berkeley, is a member of GNAM. The former dean of Haas, Richard Lyons, speaks about the power of business education to *transform* its students—to influence attitudes and character along with knowledge. He posed this question to the other deans in the network at the GNAM Summit in 2018: If students enter in state A and leave in state B, "what is it that we, as deans and directors, can be most proud of?"

In this moment, the stakes are exceedingly high for business schools and higher education in general.

Is this the opportunity for change that we have been seeking?

IDEAS WORTH TEACHING

In February 2016, Phil Knight, cofounder and chairman of Nike, granted Stanford University $400 million for a global leadership initiative. The remarkable gift supports scholarships for graduate students who plan to study and work to solve world-class problems like climate change and poverty. Knight expects his gift to be "transformative." How will Stanford assure a good return on Knight's investment?

I hope a number of the Knight scholars will apply to Stanford's business school. In spite of stereotypes about self-serving MBAs, the generation of students choosing to attend Stanford Graduate School of Business want to learn how the real world works: how to diagnose problems and design solutions, motivate employees and teams, activate a supply chain, and innovate and then measure results—to know when you are on track and when you need to try something new. Stanford GSB has relevant coursework to tackle virtually any problem.

But there is also disconnect at play: while business students enter grad school thinking like consumers and citizens—with natural curiosity about roles and relationships between and among markets, employees, host communities, and governments—our own data at Aspen shows that MBAs exit thinking more like firm-specific profit maximizers. Rather than widening their worldview, the lens inevitably *narrows* to focus on profits and share price as the most useful metric of success. When that happens, the tools for how to diagnose and fix a problem fail to sync up with the best leverage points for large-scale and systemic change—including a clear role for business and its leaders.

The grand challenges that Phil Knight's scholars will study and hope to ameliorate include complex systems, from climate change and species extinction to drought-induced mass migration and a problem that Stanford's generous donor knows well from his time at Nike: the need for globally effective human rights and labor standards. Every one of these challenges is affected by the rules of private enterprise and the business-fueled demands of consumers in developed markets.

These challenges must be studied in business schools. But to influence the long game for the vast, capacious, globe-hopping corporations, the strategies and decision rules taught in the classroom need to expand from the health of the company today to the wider ecosystem on which business depends. Managers need to analyze and understand the conditions and levers and partners for change *outside* the gate to understand the implications for their job *inside* the boardroom and C-suite.

Business educators can—must—ask fresh questions to help refocus the lens. The Saïd Business School at the University of Oxford in England engages students each year in study of "global opportunities and threats." To frame and understand the problem, students interact with alumni and other parts of the university—a great place to start.

And if business schools within elite universities continue to populate investment funds, strategy consultancies, consumer marketing programs, and the boardrooms of industry, they also need to bring along their finance classrooms, where attitudes about the purpose of the corporation are formed and the decision rules that govern investment and shape strategy are taught. To reach the next generation of leaders, the most forward-thinking scholars need to expand from coursework on sustainability and social enterprise and influence the core teachings.

Here are three questions for management educators, including finance scholars, whose students will engage in grand challenges either by choice or by necessity:

First: *What is the dominant message communicated to students about the purpose of the corporation—what do they learn?*

Investors and corporate raiders who hold sway in boardrooms expect business to attend to the share price *today*—to cut jobs and externalize costs to ensure that shareholders get their due. Phil Knight's global challenges require a much wider lens and longer time horizon than the typical decision rules are designed for.

It is critically important for finance classrooms to catch up with changes in disciplines that are better equipped to consider the human consequences of decisions, purpose, values, and business culture. The disconnect between what business schools say they stand for and what students actually *learn* can be jarring; it sends the message to the Knight scholars that they might be better off in the policy school.

Second: *What is our aim, now that "to maximum growth" no longer functions as the economic paradigm?*

For a host of reasons, the degrowth movement is finding a robust home in academia, with its own scholarly journals and conferences. Greta Thunberg, the young climate activist from Sweden, might be the most visible representative of the environmental wing of the movement, but she is only one of the important voices that are unsettling the status quo. World-renowned economists are joining the chorus.

After sailing to New York to attend the UN Climate Change Summit in fall 2019, Greta spoke forcefully to the delegates about the dominant economic policy: "We are in the beginning of a mass extinction, and all you can talk about is money and fairy tales of eternal economic growth. How dare you!" Pro-growth policy is on a collision course with biodiversity and climate change. How quickly will business classrooms catch up?

New voices and cohorts of scholars are questioning GDP growth, and not only because of planetary limit, climate change, and species decline. Nobel Prize–winning economists and a host of popular authors and pundits are asking whether growth can possibly make sense in a fully developed economy; they are revisiting GDP and the assumption of rising productivity as a useful measure.

Massive changes in consumer buying habits and greater concern for economic inequality offer even more opportunity for conscious conversation in the classroom and the public square.

Third: *What is the role of the executive, and what are the most important implements of his or her trade?*

In the aftermath of Super Tuesday 2016, Alan Murray, editor of *Fortune*, commented on the anti-business tenor of the election and shared this reflection from Jeffrey Garten, financier and former dean at the Yale School of Management:

> It would be an error of historic proportions for big business to assume . . . any new president will tack towards the center. To think that way would be grossly underestimating the degree of anger and frustration in America today. . . . Without a new grand strategy, based on a reexamination of many fundamental assumptions, America's leading global companies could find themselves facing a world that is dramatically different from the one in which they have successfully operated.[2]

What needs to be true for our belief in market-based solutions to bear out? Where does the CEO place his or her bets, and how will he or she deploy the company's extraordinary talent and problem-solving capacity?

Garten calls for business to change its tune—to move away from its focus on tax concessions, trade support, and regulatory relief for companies, and on to the grand challenges and deep public concern for the health of the system. We need business voice and commitment to change on the policy front, and we need a fresh look at the choice points in the C-suite and boardrooms to help right the ship. Progress on the grand challenges will require the best that business leaders have to offer.

The conversations taking place in B-schools now are testing a better response in classrooms when the dominant theory fails us—when the professor can no longer get away with dismissing the destructive consequences of business as usual as externalities or market failures.

No, a rising tide does not lift all boats. Yes, there are limits to growth. And enterprise success cannot be divorced from the health of the society from which business draws its strength and its customers.

These are ideas worth teaching.

◆ ◆ ◆

When I left the Ford Foundation for the Aspen Institute to focus on MBA programs, I had a plan: I would recruit six of the leading MBA programs in the United States to work with me on rethinking how business education could better prepare managers for the expanding role of corporations.

In 1998, my mantra about the work ahead went something like this: it was time to move the conversation about the impact of business on society out of the ethics classroom and into the courses that mattered most to job-seeking MBAs and recruiters—management, operations, marketing, organizational behavior, and finance.

I believed in an action-oriented, learning-by-doing approach to change. I thought the architecture of the academy would enable the best ideas and content to spread. We would focus on the movable middle to rewire classrooms that were still teaching students to externalize costs and discount the future; we would seek out teaching about stewardship and help embed the long-term consequences of business decisions into the McKinsey-esque frameworks and 2x2 matrices.

By the time the three-year grant I had received from the Ford Foundation was deposited at the Aspen Institute, I already knew the plan was deeply flawed—hopelessly naive.

The listening tour that I conducted in my last months at Ford, while I still enjoyed the Ford Foundation calling card, was illuminating. I visited a half dozen business schools, where I met with deans, students, and the easy-to-identify, go-to teacher who would empathize with my goal and confirm my analysis. This was 1997; the MBA was the degree of choice across the country. Colleges were turning out about 100,000 MBAs a year, as many as teaching credentials. Business schools were flourishing. There might be things they could do differently, but the most highly ranked schools could fill their seats many times over.

Was there really a problem?

But step by step, meeting by meeting, in partnership with insiders like Mary Gentile, a veteran of HBS, who would teach me about the motivations of scholars and the gauntlet of the tenure system, and through a fortuitous summer intern hire by the name of Claire Preisser, who joined me full-time and then built out the program, we began, through trial and error, to identify change agents and innovations to disrupt the status quo.

If rankings of business schools were principally designed to sell magazines and reward complacency, then with a formidable partner, the World Resources Institute (WRI), we could build an alternative ranking system we called *Beyond Grey Pinstripes*, to celebrate scholars asking questions about the role of business in society. Our colleague Nancy McGaw joined the team and continued to manage this complicated but impactful research program for years after WRI moved on from their work on business education.

Deans came and went, but the best left their mark at key institutions that drew students and supported scholars ready to try something new.

The organization that came to be called Net Impact, which I supported with a grant while still at the Ford Foundation, grew from a meeting of a dozen students in a living room in Santa Barbara, California, to a national conference that filled the largest convention hall in Baltimore. Local chapters on B-school campuses agitated for teaching that would prepare them for the complexity of business decision-making in a world that would come to value social and environmental stewardship.

Through these efforts and allies we identified many scholars testing new ideas and innovative curricula. The Ideas Worth Teaching Awards and a weekly digest began to elevate great teaching. Research helped us understand the impact of the classic MBA curriculum on the attitudes of students. Scholarships enticed faculty to meetings of business trade groups like Business for Social Responsibility and to numerous smaller convenings of scholars within a discipline or around a specific question. We were helping build a network of change agents and offering greater visibility for their work.

The collective work of many organizations in the United States, Europe, Africa, Asia, Latin America, and beyond; university-based centers; independent trade groups and the B-school accreditation agencies AACSB, EABIS, and the UN Principles for Responsible Management Education (PRME); and a growing number of discipline- or issue-based affinity groups within the academy itself are influencing the questions asked in business schools. All of these actions, investments, and signals conspire to mine the potential lurking on every business campus.

A NEW CONVERSATION IN BUSINESS SCHOOLS AND IN BUSINESS

The study of management and business requires a return to the fundamentals of why corporations were created to begin with: to serve critical needs and get things done that require more than individual effort or the resources of one family.

Educators take signals from the companies that employ their graduates. But as this conversation comes full circle, maybe it is time for schools, and their students, to ask questions of the recruiters. How will the company deploy the university's best graduates? Will the talent be put to good use?

We are better positioned to rebuild trust in business when the talent emerging from great universities and colleges is able to ask a future employer about the things that matter most to student-citizens:

questions about the company's philosophy about jobs and employment, surely, but also about paying taxes and how they use their voice
in Washington. How do they balance return to the shareholders today
with investment in the future of the enterprise and the host community? What are they paying their executives to do?

Is the purpose of the enterprise clear, compelling, and actionable?

The change that is taking place in businesses today signals corporate America's intention to honor its license to operate—to step
back into the public square to support the health of the commons.
In the ebb and flow of ideas in a great democracy, and in the values
that permeate the American experiment, the power and reach and
problem-solving capacities of private enterprise matter. And they
are enriched by our nation's greatest gift: remarkably diverse talent
equipped with a quality education and a growing commitment to
both business and society.

What is possible now?

◆ ◆ ◆

The slogan on a T-shirt worn by a jogger in Central Park caught my
attention: "There is no finish line."

Indeed.

None of us accomplish an important endeavor alone; we build on
the continuous flow of ideas and evidence about what works, adjust-
ing to the needs of today while anticipating the needs of those who
come after us.

The design of business and society is a continuous relay race that
will never end. But there are unmistakable signals of irreversible
forces that place us on a stronger footing than when I began this race
25 years ago. The new rules not only are written but are producing
real results—and in time to tackle the unprecedented challenges facing our world.

Notes

Chapter One: Rethinking Risk

1. Robert Horn, "Why Two Environmentally-Minded Designers Are Optimistic About the Future," *Fortune*, September 6, 2019, speech by Daan Roosegaarde, *Fortune* Global Sustainability Forum, Yunnan, China, https://fortune.com/2019/09/06/bill-mcdonough-daan-roosegaarde-climate-change-design/.

2. Chris McKnett, "The Investment Logic for Sustainability," TED Summaries, video, April 13, 2015, https://tedsummaries.com/2015/04/13/chris-mcknett-the-investment-logic-for-sustainability/.

3. Mark DesJardine and Rodolphe Durand, "Disentangling the Effects of Hedge Fund Activism on Firm Financial and Social Performance," *Strategic Management Journal* 41, issue 6 (June 2020).

4. Brian Conlan, senior economic policy adviser in Senator Baldwin's office, quoted from FactSet: "The number of activist campaigns annually has risen 60% since 2010. Last year there were 348, the most since 2008. An additional 108 were launched in this year's first quarter. Activist funds now control nearly $130 billion in assets, more than double the amount they had in 2011, according to hedge-fund tracker HFR, giving them the war chests to target even the biggest American corporations" (http://www.factset.com, accessed June 2016; page no longer available). See more: Vipal Monga, David Benoit and Theo Francis, "As Activism Rises, U.S. Firms Spend More on Buybacks Than Factories," *Wall Street Journal*, May 26, 2015.

5. Martin Lipton, "Takeover Bids in the Target's Boardroom," *Business Lawyer* 35, no. 1 (November 1979): 104.

6. Roger Martin, *Fixing the Game: Bubbles, Crashes, and What Capitalism Can Learn from the NFL* (Boston: Harvard Business Review Press, 2011).

7. Eric Motley, email to Aspen Institute staff, April 8, 2020.

8. Mortimer J. Adler and Charles Van Doren, *How to Read a Book: The Classic Guide to Intelligent Reading* (New York: Touchstone, 1940).

9. James O'Toole, *The Executive's Compass: Business and the Good Society* (New York: Oxford University Press, 1993).

10. Michael E. Porter, George Serafeim, and Mark Kramer, "Where ESG Fails," *Institutional Investor*, October 16, 2019, https://www.institutionalinvestor.com/article/b1hm5ghqtxj9s7/Where-ESG-Fails.

11. Anat R. Admati, "Rethinking Corporations and Capitalism," *Stanford GSB Experience*, June 20, 2018, https://www.gsb.stanford.edu/experience/news-history/rethinking-corporations-capitalism.

Chapter Two: The Question of Business Purpose

1. Natalie Kitroeff and David Gelles, "Claims of Shoddy Production Draw Scrutiny to a Second Boeing Jet," *New York Times*, April 20, 2019, https://www.nytimes.com/2019/04/20/business/boeing-dreamliner-production-problems.html.

2. Harvard Business Review Staff, "The Best-Performing CEOs in the World," *Harvard Business Review*, November 2015, https://hbr.org/2015/11/the-best-performing-ceos-in-the-world.

3. "Our Commitment," Business Roundtable, August 19, 2019, https://opportunity.businessroundtable.org/ourcommitment/.

4. Lynn Stout, *The Shareholder Value Myth: How Putting Shareholders First Harms Investors, Corporations, and the Public* (San Francisco: Berrett-Koehler Publishers, 2012).

Chapter Three: Responsibility Redefined

1. Speech by Phil Knight, National Press Club, Washington, DC, May 12, 1998, https://www.c-span.org/video/?c4665762/user-clip-phil-knight-1998-speech.

2. Don Tapscott and David Ticoll, *The Naked Corporation: How the Age of Transparency Will Revolutionize Business* (New York: Free Press, 2003).

3. Jason Clay, "How Big Brands Can Help Save Biodiversity," TEDGlobal 2010, video, July 2010, https://www.ted.com/talks/jason_clay_how_big_brands_can_help_save_ biodiversity?language=en.

4. Roger L. Martin, "The Virtue Matrix: Calculating the Return on Corporate Responsibility," *Harvard Business Review*, March 2002, https://hbr.org/2002/03/the-virtue-matrix-calculating-the-return-on-corporate-responsibility.

Chapter Four: The Voice of the Employee

1. Arik Hesseldahl, "Salesforce CEO Benioff Takes Stand Against Indiana Anti-Gay Law," *Vox*, March 26, 2015, https://www.vox.com/2015/3/26/11560746/salesforce-ceo-benioff-takes-stand-against-indiana-anti-gay-law.

2. Gianpiero Petriglieri, "Are Our Management Theories Outdated?" *Harvard Business Review*, June 18, 2020.

3. Gianpiero Petriglieri, "Are Our Management Theories Outdated?"

4. Clayton M. Christensen, *How Will You Measure Your Life?* (New York: Harper Business, 2012).

5. John R. Bowman, *Capitalisms Compared: Welfare, Work, and Business* (Washington, DC: CQ Press, 2013).

Chapter Five: When Capital Is No Longer Scarce

1. Marjorie Kelly, *The Divine Right of Capital: Dethroning the Corporate Aristocracy* (San Francisco: Berrett-Koehler Publishers, 2001).

2. Aric Jenkins, "Spotify's CEO Reveals Why He's Not Doing a Traditional IPO," *Fortune*, April 2, 2018, https://fortune.com/2018/04/02/spotify-ipo-daniel-ek/

3. Miguel Padró, "America's Corporate Governance System Is Racist Too," Aspen Institute Business and Society Program, June 29, 2020, https://www .aspeninstitute.org/blog-posts/americas-corporate-governance-system-is-racist-too/.

4. Speech by John Kay, "Moving Beyond 'Capitalism,'" at "Inclusive Capitalism" conference, London, March 13, 2018, https://www.johnkay.com/2018/03/13/ moving-beyond-capitalism/.

Chapter Six: When the System Is at Risk

1. Speech by William B. Benton, "The Economics of a Free Society: A Declaration of American Economic Policy," for the Committee for Economic Development, reprinted in *Fortune*, October 1944.

2. William B. Benton, "The Economics of a Free Society."

3. "Seafood Giants Join Forces to Combat Pirate Fishing," *Fish Farmer*, May 29, 2007, https://www.fishfarmermagazine.com/archive-2/seafood-giants-join-forces-to-combat-pirate-fishing-fishupdate-com/.

4. A. Espersen LLC, http://seafoodtrade.com/suppliers/a-espersen-llc.

5. Jim Cannon, email to the author, February 6, 2016, describing the illegal fishing problem in the Barents Sea and the complex, multistep process supported by Sustainable Fisheries Partnership, Greenpeace Nordic, and others to engage buyers and sellers and their industry association in collective action at the pre-competitive level, to protect the fisheries.

6. Jim Cannon, email to the author, February 6, 2016.

7. Jim Cannon.

8. Jim Cannon.

9. To better understand the need for investment and the great potential of next-generation nuclear power, read Joshua S. Goldstein and Staffan A. Qvist's book *A Bright Future: How Some Countries Have Solved Climate Change and the Rest Can Follow* (New York: PublicAffairs, 2019).

Chapter Seven: The Road Ahead: The Design of Incentives to Unlock Real Value

1. Donella H. Meadows, *Thinking in Systems: A Primer* (White River Junction, VT: Chelsea Green Publishing, 2008).

2. Marc Benioff, "We Need a New Capitalism," *New York Times*, October 14, 2019, https://www.nytimes.com/2019/10/14/opinion/benioff-salesforce-capitalism .html.

3. Kathleen McLaughlin, "A Letter from Our Chief Sustainability Officer," Wal-Mart Stores, Inc., 2016, https://cdn.corporate.walmart.com/ 3f/2d/ 7110c6954479bf5ebce64c303510/grr-3-cso-letter.pdf.

4. Anand Giridharadas, *Winners Take All: The Elite Charade of Changing the World* (New York: Knopf, 2018).

5. Nitin Nohria, "Column: Wealth and Jobs: The Broken Link," *Harvard Business Review*, November 2010, https://hbr.org/2010/11/column-wealth-and-jobs-the-broken-link.

6. Katy Milani and Irene Tung, "Curbing Stock Buybacks: A Crucial Step to Raising Worker Pay and Reducing Inequality," joint publication of National Employment Law Project (NELP) and the Roosevelt Institute, 2018, https://roo-seveltinstitute.org/curbing-stock-buybacks-crucial-step/.

7. Michael Dorff, *Indispensable and Other Myths: Why the CEO Pay Experiment Failed and How to Fix It* (Berkeley: University of California Press, 2014).

8. Anders Melin and Cedric Sam, "Wall Street Gets the Flak, but Tech CEOs Get Paid All the Money," *Bloomberg*, July 10, 2020, https://www.bloomberg.com/ graphics/2020-highest-paid-ceos/?sref=N2PD4LfX.

9. Joseph L. Bower and Lynn S. Paine, "The Error at the Heart of Corporate Leadership," *Harvard Business Review*, May–June 2017, https://hbr.org/2017/05/ managing-for-the-long-term.

Chapter Eight: Ideas Worth Teaching

1. James B. Stewart, "How Harvard Business School Has Reshaped American Capitalism," *New York Times Book Review*, April 24, 2017, https://www.nytimes .com/2017/04/24/books/review/golden-passport-duff-mcdonald.html.

2. Alan Murray, "Why Super Tuesday's Results Are Bad for Business," *Fortune*, March 2, 2016, https://fortune.com/2016/03/02/super-tuesday-business/.

Acknowledgments

I never set out to write a book.

The idea first emerged because after 15 years of leading this program, I yearned for some time to clear my head. The Rockefeller Foundation granted me a fellowship at the Bellagio Center to think about what we at the Aspen Institute Business and Society Program had learned about influencing business in pursuit of better societal and environmental outcomes. They had never hosted a fellow who worked with business, and the four weeks I spent there in late fall 2013 were nothing short of magical. I am tremendously grateful to the foundation, and to Pilar Palacia for her warm welcome and keen interest in the fellows.

It still would not have become a book without Betty Sue Flowers. We first met in Aspen in 2000 and have been collaborators on the quest to support environmentally sound and socially useful business decisions ever since. We shared a sandwich the week before I left for Bellagio, and Betty Sue asked what the book was about. As I struggled to pretend that I actually planned to write one, she interrupted with very good advice: "Don't research," she said, "just write." Her guidance then, and since, has been a true gift. She communicated a confidence that kept me moving and an uncanny ability to say just what I needed, when I needed it, to get back on the horse. Betty Sue, you are amazing.

And why it actually *is* a book is thanks to Steve Piersanti at Berrett-Koehler. We met at a conference to memorialize Lynn Stout. He was her editor and became mine. He discerned what I was trying to say, gave me a homework assignment, and wrangled an outline that put me on the right path. Thank you, Steve. And to Johanna Vondeling, who visited me a decade earlier to pitch me on writing a book then, and to all of the dedicated staff at BK, and to the reviewers who read the manuscript and offered comments, thanks.

I have already written about the importance of Lynn Stout, to whom the book is dedicated. Lynn was part of a network of thinkers and doers who shaped my passion for tackling shareholder primacy and honed our strategy across 23 years of dialogue about how to reduce the barriers to better outcomes from business.

Leo Strine's contributions to our work at the Business and Society Program are immeasurable. Bill Budinger, Sally Blount, Marty Lipton, Ira Millstein, David Langstaff, Pat Gross, Tierney Remick, Damon Silvers, Elliot Gerson, Buzz Zaino, Sam di Piazza, John Olson. Lara Warner and Krishen Mehta each have shaped my thinking and helped me, and my wonderful colleagues at Aspen BSP, to build the bridges between theory and practice that are instrumental to real change.

The countless business executives and business scholars who have offered their time and advice in pursuit of our vision have my deep thanks. My belief in business is a function of the access I have enjoyed to hundreds of teachers, researchers, managers and executives, and internal and external agents who have helped me see more clearly the pressures and tensions that hold us back and the best leverage points for change. Their candor, energy, optimism, and integrity are why I have stayed committed to this path. One individual I want to single out is Hank Schacht, who during his service as a Ford Foundation trustee and since has taught me a great deal about decision-making in public companies. He always made time for me.

I have many friends and colleagues, both from my time at the Ford Foundation and as a grantee of this remarkable institution, who provided good counsel and encouragement. Michele Kahane, who started down this road with me in 1995, and Jan Jaffe, Barry Gaberman, Frank

DeGiovanni, Hilary Pennington, and Darren Walker all deserve my thanks.

And then there is Susan Berresford, who gets her own paragraph. Susan told me to move forward when others expressed caution or concern—and then backed me up. Her friendship and mentorship over many years mean the world to me.

Lorraine Smith and Ann Graham have my deep gratitude. Their careful reading of the entire manuscript, sound critique, and clear suggestions and provocations became my bible in the editing process. Thank you. And to all of you who offered suggestions and course corrections, especially Elissa Rabellino, thank you.

To all of my colleagues and friends from the Aspen Institute and especially my fellow travelers at the Business and Society Program, this book is for you. The work that we create together is a testament to the institute's commitment to the art of dialogue and the development of leaders across sectors. I have learned, laughed, cried, and stressed out with too many of you to add all of your names here, including BSP staff who moved on to other pastures but made remarkable contributions during their tenure. You have my deepest gratitude. Dana Caryl, Nancy McGaw, Miguel Padró, Claire Preisser—thank you for the unique and specific ways that you have each enriched this journey. I hope you are as proud of what we have built together as I am, and that the book is of use.

And last, but assuredly not least, to my family—especially my husband, Vic, who has weathered way too many vacations and early mornings committed to writing, and whose unconditional support enabled me to keep swimming hard. Babe, after 36 years of marriage you can still make me laugh; you mean the world to me. And to my children, Sarah and Anna, and son-in-law Chris; my siblings and nieces; and especially my sister-in-law Beth, who was my biggest cheerleader from the very beginning. I can't thank you all enough for your love and patience and support.

Index

About the Author

Judy Samuelson is the executive director of the Aspen Institute's Business and Society Program and a vice president of the institute, where she focuses on leveraging the power of business and its leaders to advance the health of the commons. She has worked at the forefront of fresh thinking about the purpose of business for more than 25 years.

The Aspen Business and Society Program, which she founded in 1998 with a three-year grant from the Ford Foundation, has three objectives: to broaden teaching in business schools about the purpose of corporations; to build the courage, conviction, and capacity of change agents in the world of business; and to shift the narrative about the role and purpose of business—i.e., bring an end to shareholder primacy and prioritize long-term thinking. Signature programs include the First Movers Fellowship for social intrapreneurs and the Aspen Leaders Forum, a network of senior corporate responsibility and sustainability strategists influencing the future of the profession.

Multiyear, multisector engagements and dialogues led by Judy gave rise to the Aspen Principles for Long-Term Value Creation on curbing short-termism in business and capital markets (2007), the American Prosperity Project on policy to reward long-term investment (2016), and Modern Principles for Sensible and Effective Executive Pay to guide board conversations on the integrity of pay in light of the changing role of the CEO (2020).

Judy is a native Californian, born and raised in San Diego County. After attending UCLA, she worked in legislative affairs in Sacramento and then moved east to attend business school at the Yale School of Management, where she made friends for a lifetime. She worked as a commercial banker in New York's Garment Center before taking a dream job at the Ford Foundation, where she ran the Office of Program-Related Investments, a $150 million social impact fund invested in affordable housing, micro-enterprise, and economic development in the United States and parts of the developing world— India, Bangladesh, and Mexico. In 1994, with a nudge from foundation trustees, she launched the Corporate Involvement Initiative, a comprehensive effort to encourage partnerships for economic development and leverage business investment to strengthen communities.

Judy blogs for Quartz at Work, and she is a director of the Financial Health Network and a Rockefeller Foundation Fellow. She is past president and a deacon of the Unitarian Church of All Souls, is passionate about the town of Gosport on Star Island, and cherishes her time as an AFS exchange student in Sardinia, Italy. Judy lives in New York with her husband of 36 years, Vic Henschel, and has two adult children, Anna and Sarah.

Berrett–Koehler
Publishers

Berrett-Koehler is an independent publisher dedicated to an ambitious mission: *Connecting people and ideas to create a world that works for all.*

Our publications span many formats, including print, digital, audio, and video. We also offer online resources, training, and gatherings. And we will continue expanding our products and services to advance our mission.

We believe that the solutions to the world's problems will come from all of us, working at all levels: in our society, in our organizations, and in our own lives. Our publications and resources offer pathways to creating a more just, equitable, and sustainable society. They help people make their organizations more humane, democratic, diverse, and effective (and we don't think there's any contradiction there). And they guide people in creating positive change in their own lives and aligning their personal practices with their aspirations for a better world.

And we strive to practice what we preach through what we call "The BK Way." At the core of this approach is *stewardship,* a deep sense of responsibility to administer the company for the benefit of all of our stakeholder groups, including authors, customers, employees, investors, service providers, sales partners, and the communities and environment around us. Everything we do is built around stewardship and our other core values of *quality, partnership, inclusion,* and *sustainability.*

This is why Berrett-Koehler is the first book publishing company to be both a B Corporation (a rigorous certification) and a benefit corporation (a for-profit legal status), which together require us to adhere to the highest standards for corporate, social, and environmental performance. And it is why we have instituted many pioneering practices (which you can learn about at www.bkconnection.com), including the Berrett-Koehler Constitution, the Bill of Rights and Responsibilities for BK Authors, and our unique Author Days.

We are grateful to our readers, authors, and other friends who are supporting our mission. We ask you to share with us examples of how BK publications and resources are making a difference in your lives, organizations, and communities at www.bkconnection.com/impact.

Dear reader,

Thank you for picking up this book and welcome to the worldwide BK community! You're joining a special group of people who have come together to create positive change in their lives, organizations, and communities.

What's BK all about?

Our mission is to connect people and ideas to create a world that works for all.

Why? Our communities, organizations, and lives get bogged down by old paradigms of self-interest, exclusion, hierarchy, and privilege. But we believe that can change. That's why we seek the leading experts on these challenges—and share their actionable ideas with you.

A welcome gift

To help you get started, we'd like to offer you a **free copy** of one of our bestselling ebooks:

www.bkconnection.com/welcome

When you claim your **free ebook**, you'll also be subscribed to our blog.

Our freshest insights

Access the best new tools and ideas for leaders at all levels on our blog at ideas.bkconnection.com.

Sincerely,

Your friends at Berrett-Koehler

Certified

Corporation